IMAGES
of Wales

FROM ROCH TO RAMSEY
THE ST DAVID'S
PENINSULA

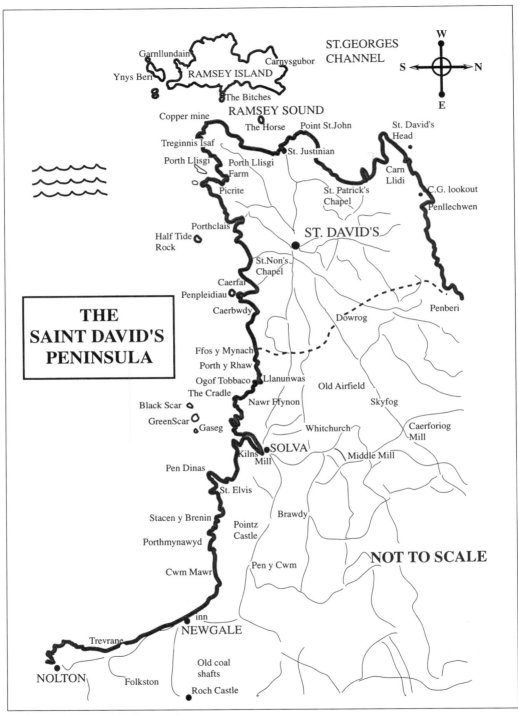

A sketch of St David's Peninsula.

IMAGES
of Wales

FROM ROCH TO RAMSEY
THE ST DAVID'S
PENINSULA

Compiled by
Paul Raggett MBE RD

TEMPUS

First published 1999
Copyright © Paul Raggett, 1999

Tempus Publishing Limited
The Mill, Brimscombe Port,
Stroud, Gloucestershire, GL5 2QG

ISBN 0 7524 1805 X

Typesetting and origination by
Tempus Publishing Limited
Printed in Great Britain by
Midway Clark Printing, Wiltshire

Further Reading

An Historical Tour through Pembrokeshire	Richard Fenton
History of Solva	F.W. Warburton
Solva Saga	Eric Freeman
The Pembrokshire Explorer	Roger Worsley
Lighthouses	Douglas B. Hague and Rosemary Christie
A Portrait of Pembrokeshire	Dillwyn Miles
Pembrokeshire Sea Trading before 1990	Barbara George
St David's and Dewisland	David James
The Pembrokeshire Coast Footpath	John Barratt
The Pembrokeshire Coast National Park Handbook	The Park Authority
Pembrokeshire	Brian John
A Description of Pembrokeshire	George Owen
History of Solva	Trevor Broom
History and Guide to St David's	Henry Rvans
The Footsteps of our Fathers	Peter B.S. Davies
Dai the Mill	D.J. Lewis
Forgotten Mines	Peter B.S. Davies
History and Antiquities of St David's	Jones and Freeman
History and Antiquities of the Parish of St David's	Peter B.S. Davies

Contents

Acknowledgements

I am most grateful to the many people who helped to compile this 'photographic history' of the St David's Peninsula, there have been so may that I sincerely hope that I have not left anyone out; if this happens to be the case I am very sorry, I only hope that this collection gives as much enjoyment to the readers as it did to me when I called on people I had not seen for some years. Thanks to my wife Jean, Penny and Mathew for their patience and their help in editing and checking the captions. Thanks to Nigel Barrah whose cheerful enthusiasm was responsible for reproducing the photographs and Trish Young for sorting out disagreements between me and the word processor. The compilation of the contents of the book was only made possible by those who kindly loaned their photographs and searched their memories for the dates of the photographs and the names of those included in them. My thanks to Dr William Evans, Penny Ward, Richard and Jane Pascoe, Elwyn Davies, Glyn Phillips, Alun Phillips, Derek Huyton, Dr George Middleton, Len James, Alun James, Chris Martin, Margaret and Grahame Canby-Lewis, Jean Davies (née Watkins), Brian John, Peggy Evans, Ruth Davies, Dr Peter and Janet Thomas, Dai John, Grace Scott (née Lloyd), Megan Jones (née Evans), Yvonne Rees (née Thomas), Avril Philpott, Derek Ward, Irene Waters, Willie and Jan Phillips, Graham Salmon, Beti Lewis, Edward Coles, David James, Anne White, Eunice Smith, Grace Davies, Peter Voyce, Jim Hickman, Colin Jacob, Patricia Murphy, Peter Williams, The Maritime Heritage Museum, Keith Dufton, Roy Watkins, Peter Davies, Nora Nash, Jim Canton, George Harries, Nancy Bayly, John Evans (Studio John), Tiv Thomas, The Pembrokeshire Coast National Park, Terry Roach, Bill and Ron Owens, Rex Davies, Jamie King, John Arter, Robert Driver, The St David's Historical Society, The St David's Assemblies, Dai Lewis (the Mill), D.G. Hampson, Gwyneth Davies, Barrett Lee, Peter Lewis, Idwal Chapman, George Harries, Ceinwin Richards, Mattie Williams, Ian Bullock, John Rogers, Robert Lewis, Rowland Jones, Mel Calder, Gordon Cawood, Eric Hemingway, David Bennett, Martin Roberts, Ruth James, Haverfordwest Record Office and Library, Mary John, The National Trust, Scolton Museum, St Fagan's Folk Museum, Ruth Barker, Nona Rees, Rosina Gray, Captain Jim Arnold, K. Anthony Ellis, HM Coastguard Museum, Joy Church. I have made every effort to recall and spell all the names correctly. Some of the photographs have been left out for reasons of editing – once again my apologies.

Introduction

In 1931, as we were quite a large family, my father decided that rather than spend two weeks holiday in some boarding house by the sea, it would be far more sensible to find a cottage in the country. This is how we found ourselves, on a drizzly, damp, April day in the early thirties, sitting on the harbour wall at Saundersfoot looking at a ketch across the harbour loading coal under the gantry. For some reason we were not very impressed by this industrial scene, so we returned to the car and continued our journey westward.

The mist of time descends, and I know not how we arrived on the road to St David's, but the unforgettable view is indelible on the mind. As the road winds down to Newgale, the great panorama of St Brides Bay suddenly appears, an ever-changing scene that always impresses the many visitors that come to the west coast of Wales.

Passing through Solva one has a glimpse of the harbour as the road rises to the upper village. Opposite to where the village pump once was, adjacent to the Memorial Hall, it turns left and the traveller is carried on past the present post office and down a steep lane, overlooking the harbour. It was here that we had our picnic, the sun came out and we were in paradise. We came down for the summer, we came down for Easter, we came down for Christmas, we came down forever!

Paul Raggett
Solva 1998

The St David's Peninsula from the cliffs to the south west of Newgale.

One
Roch, Nolton and Newgale

An early photograph of Nolton Haven.

On entering the St David's Peninsula two outstanding landmarks are visible. In the far distance are the hills of Penberi and Carn Llidi. Inland is a rock outcrop on which Adam de la Rupe built Roch Castle. Legend has it that a curse was put on the family, that the first born would be bitten by a snake. One day, while collecting firewood for the nursery, the servant did not see a snake crawl into the basket, thus the curse came to pass. On a visit to this area in 1791, the diarist Mary Morgan describes how she was fearful of walking the district 'lest she should stumble into a coal pit', and that the 'coal mines extend a prodigious way under the earth. There are almost as many women who work in the mines as men'.

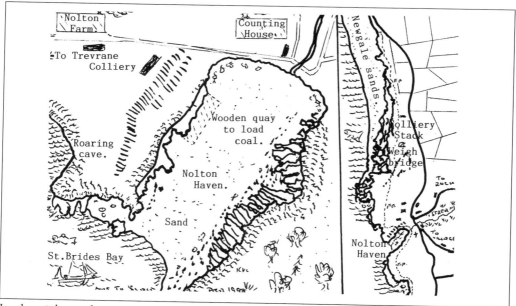

In the eighteenth century, a seam of anthracite was discovered that crossed St Brides Bay, coming ashore between Newgale and Little Haven, crossing Pembrokeshire to Saundersfoot and eventually reaching the valleys of South Wales. Historian George Owen forecast a great industrial future for the area and even Queen Victoria ordered that this coal should be used in her Royal Navy. Unfortunately the heat generated was such that it burned out the fire bars! Nearby Nolton Haven was one of the ports from which coal was exported. According to veteran inhabitant, Barrett Lee, a wooden quay was constructed to enable visiting vessels to load from the nearby mines.

The Ketch *Mary Ann* came to grief in a great gale in 1905 and, with the heavy baulks of timber on the beach, it would look as though the wooden quay fell to the fury of the storm at the same time. This part of the hamlet has not changed much since this photograph taken in 1906.

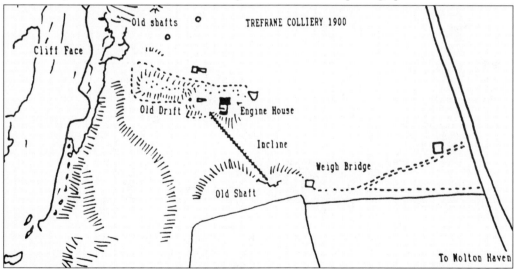

Situated between Newgale and Nolton, the remains of the coal stack of the pump house of Trefrane Colliery can easily be seen from the road. There is an apocryphal tale that in 1905 the engineer over indulged at the local Victoria Inn on a Saturday night. When he arrived for work on Monday the mine was flooded and subsequently closed. The drawing also shows the tramway where the coal was hauled up to the weighbridge.

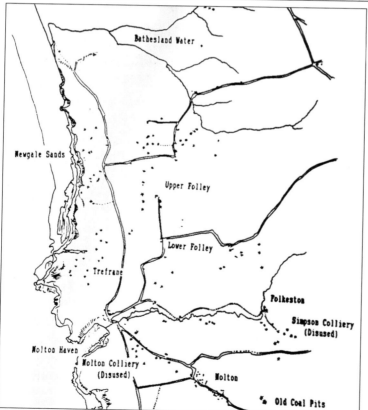

When coal was initially discovered in the Nolton area in the middle part of the eighteenth century, the miners worked in what were known as 'bell pits', and as can be seen from the drawing the men would have to dig down to the seam and work outwards. They would presumably continue until the overhang became too unsafe and then they would start all over again. It was the job of the women and children to wind up the baskets of coal.

This sketch shows the distribution of pits in the district, c. 1891.

The stack of the Trefrane mine is alongside the ruin of the pump house just above the mineshaft. It was built by the grandfather of 'Tom' Thomas, late of St David's. The lower part was masonry while the higher section was built with the bricks that were made by the Llethr Estate brickworks which were at the bottom of Cwm Mawr Valley, below Pen-y-cwm.

To the right of the stack was an incline where the coal was transported to the top of the slope to be weighed before being taken away.

Paul Blick (right) of the Pembrokeshire Coast National Park created the 180-mile footpath from Amroth to Poppet sands and is seen with Voluntary Warden Jean Raggett above Newgale Beach.

The Bridge Inn at Newgale, seen around 1893, was on the sea side of the road, but it succumbed to a great gale in 1897. As a boy William Henry Davies, a shipwright from Solva, was sitting on the side of the hill on the east side of the beach when the inn was overcome by the ferocity of the storm. He watched as the licensee Mrs Allen was rescued by a horse and trap. Mrs Allen had the public house rebuilt on the other side of the road. The Royal Coat of Arms can be seen incorporated in the sign, as the then Duke of Edinburgh had called on his way to St David's, the name was changed to commemorate the royal visit.

14

The Bridge Inn is seen here around 1953 with Jack Williams (second left) standing alongside the licensee Tom Walters (left). Mrs Walters, affectionately known as 'Aunty Mag', can be seen in the doorway behind Tom's brother Jack with his wife Kitty Walters. They farmed Trefrane Farm where a coal mine was once worked. In 1963, the farmer was Adrian John and one day he went out shooting with his brother when his dog fell down one of the old ventilation shafts. He contacted the Royal Navy at Brawdy who came to his aid and rescued the dog, who seemed no worse for the experience.

Newgale certainly has its fair share of flooding with heavy rainfall, a spring tide and south westerly gales which meant that the pebbles tended to pile up at the outlet of the stream, thus building up the water behind. The stream is called Brandy Brook, which is perhaps a corruption of Brawdy; it is also part of the dividing line which crosses to south Pembrokeshire called the 'Landsker', which is supposed to divide the Welsh speaking area from 'Little England beyond Wales'.

The bungalow to the left was built by Colonel Massey for his mother for £400 just after the First World War. The quarry on the hill was owned by the Watts family of Pontpren Farm, just across the valley, and was worked until 1934. The cows are probably from Newgale Farm, just on the brow of the hill. Newgale has not changed a lot since this photograph was taken around 1922.

The Radio Location masts can still be seen on the right above Trefrane Farm just after the Second World War, c. 1947. The three were made of wood blew down in a gale in 1953, while the metal ones remained standing, to be removed at a later date. RAF Folly was built in 1941 to plot enemy action and the 'active' part of the station was located by the masts. The messes and residential area were where the Roch Gate Motel is now, the air-raid shelter is still there! The name Folly was taken from two smallholdings that no longer exist.

On 2 February 1944 an airfield was built above Newgale, inland from the main road to St David's. The road can be seen as a line across the top of the photograph. Initially the airfield had grass runways and was a satellite to St David's airfield which was built earlier. On 1 November 1945 the order was reversed and Brawdy became the master airfield due to the fact that the runways were better oriented to the prevailing winds.

The Royal Navy took RAF Brawdy over in January 1946, with 811 Squadron, which was the first Sea Mosquito Squadron. Flying training was carried out here as well as flying for the Night Fighter School established at Dale. In August 1947 the station was reduced to care and maintenance but was re-commissioned in September 1952 with the Seahawks of 806 Squadron. The station was returned to the RAF in 1971 to be replaced by the 14th Signal Regiment in 1996 and has now became Cawdor Barracks. The removal of the search and rescue facility that had been provided by Brawdy for forty-nine years was a serious loss to the coastal community. Here, a Westland Whirlwind XL846 is practising off Pen Dinas.

U.S. NAVAL FACILITY BRAWDY

DISESTABLISHMENT
CEREMONY

U.S. NAVAL FACILITY

DIM LLOCHES YN Y DYFNDER

BRAWDY

1974 - 1995

As the Cold War was a cause of some concern in the late 1960s, NATO decided that as the US Navy had maintained a programme of oceanographic surveys, a base should be established at Brawdy. In November 1971 an agreement was reached between Britain and America resulting in the construction of a US Naval Facility which became operational in 1974. A cable was laid under the base, under the road to St David's and entered the sea at Cwm Mawr, below Pen-y-cwm. It is understood that the equipment used was so sensitive that it could even identify different species of marine mammals.

The US Naval Facility crest was designed to depict the co-operation between the two countries. The American Eagle is on top of a fouled anchor with the golden lions rampant with the Welsh Red Dragons passant. In the centre is the Technicians Rating Badge – Neptune's Trident. The Welsh translation reads 'No sanctuary in the deep.'

Two
Solva

Solva village and harbour, *c.* 1908.

The Fox Hunt meet on Solva foreshore, *c.* 1880. The house immediately behind was known as The Academy and navigation was taught in the room upstairs. In the early part of the nineteenth century there were about thirty locally owned boats working out of the harbour. Two ketches were built in the area around 1810: the 110-ton *Royal George* and the 115-ton *Charlotte*. Just behind the Solva Academy was where Henry Whiteside lived; he was the builder of the first Smalls Lighthouse.

A photograph of Henry Evans with his mother in 1916 and portraits of her parents on the wall behind. Henry Evans had a showcase of the wild birds of the district, which he had caught and stuffed. He presented them with a background of their natural habitats. He also made a superb model of the two lighthouses that had been built in Solva and erected on the Hats and Barrels Reef. Both he and Lord St David's were staunch Liberals, and the peer was heard to say one day to a friend that Henry, 'was the only man he knew who could drop a pair of woodcock with a left and right barrel'!

These were the 'City Fathers' of Solva in 1926. W.H. John JP, of the Guardian Office, carried out his civic duties alongside a printing business using the original printing equipment that had been used to print the local paper and now printed posters and notices. To the left is Samson Williams of Tan-yr-Allt, whose family had been involved in the business side of shipping and agriculture. The family have had a significant effect on the area, not least because it was his brother Richard who, in 1937, gave the land bordering the harbour to the National Trust. There is a memorial stone recording this event at the top of the Gribin path, opposite the quay. On the right is ornithologist, writer and historian Henry Evans JP of Harbour House.

Around 1906, when one of the richest men in the country Viscount Rhondda visited Solva, the sight of a motor car was a rarity. According to Cliff Robertson of the Pembrokeshire Motor Museum, this one is a French made Panhard-Lenessor. Also in the photograph are Henry Evans in front of the doorway and PC Thomas Nash who was in Solva from 1904 to 1907.

When the 'new' footbridge to the Gribin was built in 1929 it was an event of some importance to the village. Henry Evans JP is seen leading the way and is receiving a salute form Solva's Customs and Excise Officer Holloway and PC Thomas facing him, with his back to the camera. Henry Evans is being followed by B.J. Lewis, chairman of the Parish Council and Morris Lewis who was responsible for building the bridge is looking on from the steps on the left.

William Thomas and his wife Mary Ann were the two proprietors of the Mariner's Store in Main Street. In the pre-war years, rabbit catching provided a very important industry in Pembrokeshire. There was a rail link between Fishguard and Rosebush which was kept going because of the demand. William is seen in Prendergast with his pony and trap and his dog Chance around 1928. Miss Davies can be seen in the doorway of her shop Golden Grove.

Francis Calighan was a remarkable character in the early part of the twentieth century. He had a 'string' of donkeys with which he journeyed to Trefrane and Folkeston coal mines near Nolton for anthracite dust, known as culm. The culm was delivered around the houses where it was the task of the children to mix it with clay into balls which were stacked outside the back door ready for the kitchen fire. This smokeless fuel burned well and would be stoked up at night so that in the following morning a hole was poked down through the culm which had the kettle boiling very soon. Calighan is outside Gwalia House, with the shop of C.M. Rees the tailor and photographer next to Prance the post office.

In the years that followed the First World War the last but one house in River Street belonged to Jack and Meena Nicholas. Jack was not only the village tailor but was also well known as a choirmaster and conducted choirs in Neyland, St David's and Solva. As can be seen in the photograph he was as successful a choirmaster as he was tailor – it is only natural that he specialized in Middle Mill cloth!

From the left: Tom Wetherby came to Solva to visit his friend Peter Voyce at the Ship Inn in 1958. Alongside Peter is a ftsherman, Wynford 'Sharkey' Phillips, who a few years later became the harbourmaster. Making a point is Solva's butcher Jim Davies with William Thomas of the Mariners Store from over the road who was one time landlord of the Ship.

Before mains water was brought to Solva, in 1937, it was the women and children who carried water from the wells and pumps in the village. This lady would be on her way to the pump opposite the Memorial Hall. The field on the right was part of Panteg Farm where there is now an access road into the development that took place in the 1960s known as Anchor Down. Just above on the right is Mount Pleasant Baptist chapel which was built, in 1863, to replace the smaller chapel to accommodate the increasing membership.

The pump was the regular meeting place and it was usual to sit on the wall and discuss village affairs. Here is Mike Thomas with his friend Rowland Waters whose parents owned the adjoining shop in 1953. All that remains today to indicate where the pump once was is the telephone kiosk.

The front of the Memorial Hall is part of the original building and was constructed as a Wesleyan chapel in 1812. It was later leased, and partially re-built by the Harries family of Llanunwas as a 'commemorative establishment' to those lost in the First World War. The foundation stone was laid on Armistice Day in 1921 and the unveiling ceremony took place on the 12 May 1938. Inside there are two plaques commemorating the fallen in the two world wars. Just below is the Swan Café which was kept by Ivor Williams and his housekeeper Mrs Linstrom.

A little further up the road, opposite St Aidan's church, was the village pond which was called Pwll Melin and has since been filled in and is now a car park complete with public lavatory. Emrys Evans and Patricia Harries are seen here in 1932, collecting Jim Evans' cows which are having a drink before milking time. Cecily Davies, a botanist from Haverfordwest, would regularly visit the pond as she would find very rare wild plants there.

Members of the first troupe of Solva Girl Guides in 1929 are, left to right, standing: Francis Williams and Megan Evans. Seated: Phyllis Howells, Betty Evans, Letty May Davies, Dorothy Griffith, Mrs Rowe (the captain), Betty Evans from the vicarage, Irene Beynon, Emma Williams. Sat on the ground: Nella Davies, Rhoda Stephens, Florence Davies, Grace Lloyd, Elfair Thomas, Freda Field, Molly Griffiths, Betty Griffiths.

This is the first troupe of Solva Girl Guides outside the Memorial Hall in 1937. Left to right, back row: Violet Harries, Olive George, Gwyneth Davies, Margaret Morris, Hilda Reynolds, Gracie Davies. Middle row: Irene Waters, R. Evans, Dorothy Holloway, Eileen Thomas, Beti Lewis, Jenny Jenkins, Peggy Jenkins, Eunice Gronow, Patty Evans, Beryl George, Grace Lloyd. Front row: T. Evans, Ceinwen Rees, Mavis George, Mrs Algy Mathias, Lady Merthyr, Dorothy Griffiths, Eirlys Davies, May Roberts, Margaret Palmer.

In 1924 the newly formed Solva Women's Institute had their outing to Newgale. Back row includes: Mrs J. Jenkins, Mrs Davies (Moelfro), Nancy Lewis, Addi Prance, Emma Harries, Mrs W.H. John, Mrs Prance, Mrs Holloway, Connie Prance. Front includes: Florence Davies, Freda Field, Grace Lloyd, Elfair Thomas, Kate George and Rhysted, Maud John, Mrs G.H. Lloyd, Tilley George and others.

To celebrate the 75th birthday of the Solva Women's Institute, in 1992, a tree was planted in Parc-y-Capel, Solva's Village Green. Planting the tree are, left to right: Mary Clifford, Jean Platt, and Margaret Phillips, and in the background are: Dorothy Griffiths, Joyce Clark, Iris Morgan, Edna Eastham, Marjorie Swan, Rosemary Gillam, Diana Monte, Judith Neuman.

Main Street, Solva, in 1906. On the left is Moelfro, now Window on Wales. The house under the sign 'Perth Dye', became Tom Roach's Cycle Shop. In the house next door the *Pembroke County Guardian* and *Cardigan Reporter* were still being printed, and next door was Mariner's, a general store known as the 'Gin Shop'. Outside the warehouse at the end of Main Street, owned by the Williams family of Tan-yr-allt, the men are loading corn into a cart to be loaded on the ships waiting in the harbour. At the far end, on the bridge, is Miss Tousdale's shop, now no more. On the right is the drapery shop, owned by Phillips of Mathry, the Ship Inn and Prance the post office.

Forty-six years later, in 1952, the grain warehouses have been converted into flats and the warehouse immediately on the left is a tea shop. Tom Roach, as well as selling bicycles is also selling petrol. The *Guardian Newspaper* has been sold to the Hammond family of Haverfordwest, but W.H. John still carries on printing local notices with the help of typesetter Jim Davies. The notice over the door announces that once a week it is Lloyds Bank! On the right is Gwryd House, with the garage and transport business of Morris Lewis.

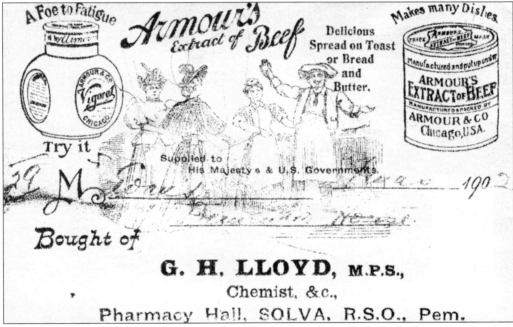

'Lloyd the Chemist' was the 'centre' of the village where almost everything could be bought; it also operated as the post office with five postmen and telegram 'boy' as well as the telephone exchange with a young lady sitting at the switchboard. It was here that medicines were dispensed together with postcards, chocolate, paint and sundry goods. Apart from his business G.H. Lloyd was also involved with many of the organizations of the village.

G.H. Lloyd and Bernie Thomas are seen here outside the pharmacy in 1931. Bernie was the son of Captain Osbourne Thomas and after serving as a Surgeon Lieutenant in the Royal Navy during the war became a GP in Bury St Edmunds.

In 1949 it was decided to hold a party for the senior citizens in the Memorial Hall. Left to right, back row: Nansi Davies, I. Rees, T. Evans, Holloway the Customs Officer, Phillips of Tremaenhir, Edwin Harries, Peter Griffiths, William Henry Davies, Walla John, Basil Davies. Middle row: Willie Owen, M. Reynolds, Alice James, W. John, N. Reynolds, Sarah Owen, Polly Davies, Maggie Thomas, Mrs Roberts, Mrs Jenkins Caerfarchell, Maud John, Bill Owens. Front row: Iris Beer, the minister the Revd I. Thomas, Bessie Nicholas, Mrs 'Captain' Jenkins, Mrs Holloway, Mrs Davies 'Moelfro', Mrs John, Blodwen Davies, the chairman of the Council Willie Thomas.

These were the ladies present at a meeting of the Felinganol chapel sisterhood in 1973. Left to right, back row: Ray Williams, Mrs Mills with young Clive, Dora Rees, Lizzie Reynolds, Mrs Lloyd (Felinganol Corn Mill), Gertie Walters, Sara Walters, Ezer Rees, -?-, Mrs Evans (the Durham), Mrs Reynolds (Middle Mill), Mrs Dai Reynolds, Mrs Willie Thomas, Mary Ann Thomas. Front row, seated: Eufron Baker, Mrs Rees, Mrs E.J. Williams (the Manse), Bessie Davies.

In a note to his sister, in 1935, Ivor Williams enclosed a 'snap' taken outside the Bay Hotel of three of Solva's oldest residents. The note read: 'Many thanks for your letter, I enclose a snap of the three oldest males in Solva. Will Ami 94, Self 83, Holloway 74. Yours Sincerely Ivor.' The three men are: retired Customs Officer Edward Percy Holloway (left) and Ivor Williams who ran Swan Café with his housekeeper Mrs Lindsrom. Will 'Ami' Davies is sat in front.

Four of the characters of the village, left to right: Meyrick Watson, Jack Evans, Ted Gavin and John Phillips, outside the Royal George, *c.* 1970. The 'Bay' was built by Captain Moses Cormack, the great great grandfather of the late Sara Rowe of Caeegwyn in 1815. He brought timber back from the Baltic for the building of a house called 'The Prospect' after his ship. The house was later divided into two and called Ye Steppes. In the early 1940s Roy Fletcher, who was tenant of the Royal George a few doors down at No. 9 High Street, asked his landlord, who also owned Ye Steppes, if he could move up the street which he did and changed the name to The Bay Hotel. In 1969 the property was bought and the new landlord decided to revert to the old name, so once again there was a Royal George.

An early picture of Solva school with W.D. Evans inset. He owned the *Redwing* a small dinghy built in Pembroke Dock before the First World War in which he also taught seamanship. In the magazine *Sea Breezes* dated 21 April 1921 (cost 2p) under the heading 'Fine Little School in Distant Pembrokeshire' the writer referred to training lads for the sea, and how it was quite remarkable that six old boys were Master Mariners in the Canadian Pacific Steamship Company. How many others there were sailing with the other lines is not known, but the article concludes with, 'not a bad record of a village with 400 inhabitants'!

The National School was opened in 1834. In 1844 there was one master, who was paid £138 per annum and occupied a house in the grounds. He had an assistant teacher and three monitors, older children who helped, and there were eighty-five children on the roll. In 1881 it amalgamated with the Congregational School and was administered by the Whitchurch (Solva) Board. After the First World War it had a facelift and the walls were made higher.

In 1924 the pupils at the school were, left to right, back row: Billy Christmas Evans, Will Jones, Harri Williams, John Howells, Meurig Vaughan, Ieuan Evans, Verdun Williams. Middle row: Megan George, -?-, Anita Vaughan, Millie Griffiths, Annie Thomas, Molly Griffiths, Eirwen Harries, Ada Gronow, Mabel Morgan, Elfair Thomas. Front row, kneeling: Colwyn Vaughan, -?-, Islwyn Williams, Alun Young, Tom Griffiths, -?-, Gwyn Prickett, Norman John, Jim Hughes.

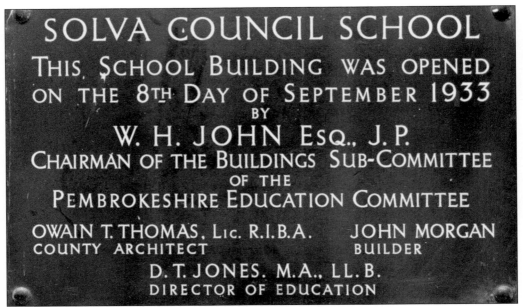

SOLVA COUNCIL SCHOOL

THIS SCHOOL BUILDING WAS OPENED
ON THE 8TH DAY OF SEPTEMBER 1933
BY
W. H. JOHN Esq., J.P.
CHAIRMAN OF THE BUILDINGS SUB-COMMITTEE
OF THE
PEMBROKESHIRE EDUCATION COMMITTEE

OWAIN T. THOMAS, Lic. R.I.B.A.   JOHN MORGAN
COUNTY ARCHITECT   BUILDER

D. T. JONES. M.A., LL. B.
DIRECTOR OF EDUCATION

The New Council School was built on Llanungar Lane in upper Solva and opened by the chairman of the Parish Council, W.H. John JP, on the 8 September 1933. Gwilym Lewis became the new headmaster and after thirty-nine years remarkable service to the village W.D. Evans retired.

At the outbreak of war, in 1939, the pupils and staff mustered outside for the school photograph. Left to right, back row: Gwylym Lewis (headmaster), Willie Davies (his assistant), then Gwilym Davies, Norman Price, Ivan Evans, Noel Davies, Bryn Rees, Vivian Jenkins, Raymond Reynish, Trevor Howells, Douglas Phillips, David John, Mildred Thomas and Letty May Davies (teachers). Second row from the back: Beryl Evans, Joyce Evans, Eleanor Evans, Ruby Thomas, Mavis George, Olive Reynolds, Gwen Morris, Lily Evans, Martha Rees, May Roberts, Peggy Evans, Nan Reynolds, Eirlys Davies. Third row: Dewi Phillips, Eddie George, Cecil Parkins, Iris Howells, Kathleen Davies, Dorothy Evans, Zita Davies, Pat Perkins, Pamela Gronow, Gwennie George, Joan Morris, Edna Williams, Bryan John, Joe Evans, Malcolm Carruthers. Front row, kneeling: Oscar Price, Gordon Morgan, David George, Jack Jenkins, John Davies, Jack Richards, Gerald Phillips, Brynach Davies, I. Morris, John Howells, John Evans, Terry Davies, Malcom Reynolds, John Evans.

With the outbreak of war there was a mass evacuation of children from London and in 1940 the pupils of Tumbleys Road School arrived in the village complete with their headmaster, and they were accommodated in and around the village. The two headmasters were Gwilym Lewis and F.W. Warburton MA (London) who also wrote a very good history of Solva starting from the ice age. He wrote it for his senior class with the help of two local residents, Solva born Richard Williams, headmaster of Cowbridge Grammar School and Dr Felix Oswald PhD.

In this photograph of Solva County Primary School infants' class, around 1957, are the two teachers, Miss Rita Davies and Mrs M. Lewis (seated). The pupils are, left to right, back row: Beryl John, Carol Davies, Kevin Evans, Alan Edwards, David Howells, Simon Lewis, Kelvin Jenkins. Second row from the back: Derek James, David Davies, Fred Morris, David Harries, Clive Mills, Margaret Evans, Brian Harries. Third row: Nesta Reynolds, Anona John, Sally Davies, Moira Morgan, Ann Fletcher, Carolyn Phillips, Bernard Mathias, Phillip Lewis. Front row, seated: John Rees, Phillip Rees, Penny Raggett, Alison Thomas, Yvonne Phillips, Phillip Bowen.

In this view of Solva County Primary School in 1956 are, left to right, back row: Barry Davies, Terry Richards, Ian John, Alan Jenkins, Lawson Morgan, Donald Young, Arthur Phillips, Leslie James (headmaster). Middle row: Victor Reynolds, Arnold Evans, Malcolm James, Gareth Jenkins, David Rees, Owain Lewis, John Griffiths, Richard Pugh, Richard Mathias. Front row, seated: June Taylor, Susan Price, Gloria Davies, Carol Jones, Margaret Evans, Jean James, Rhian Williams, Elizabeth Richards, Karen Ellison, Janet Perkins, Marion Davies.

The Solva Under 15 football team, 1972/3. Left to right, back row: George Durham, Colin Reynolds, Peter Thomas, David Flanagan, Colwyn Davies, Paul Roach. Front row, seated: Ian Walsh, Nolan Phillips, Huw George, Adrian Richards, Nicholas Bennett, Huw Reynolds, Steven Strohman.

With the help of Mrs Prickett, Llanddinog, Mrs B.J. Lewis, Jim Mills and Morris Mendus, Mrs Percy Beer produced a pantomime *The Snow Queen* which took place at the City Hall, St David's, on the 9 February 1951. Here, Norma Beer as the Snow Queen is surrounded by her fairies. Left to right, back row: Christine Gould, Elizabeth John, Ray Morris, Elizabeth Morgan, Jane Saunders, Norma Beer, Sandra Freeman, -?-, Dorothy Phillips, Doreen Williams, Maureen Childs, Margaret Lewis, Diane Wareing. Front row: Joan Eades, Angela Mills, Ann Phillips, Yvonne Davies, Hazel John, Christine Owens.

In this classroom scene is jester Barbara Perkins holding the horse with Bill Owens as Lord Felinganol. At the back are: Nesta Phillips, Marion Phillips, Patricia Beer, Jean Davies, Peter Lewis, Cynthia Griffiths, Sylvia Perkins, Wendy Fletcher, William Saunders, Neville Perkins, Huw Thomas, Drusilia John, Elwyn John, the Dunce Derek John. The teacher is Eric Hemingway. Front row: Anthony Glave, Julien Fletcher, Colin Mills, Raymond Vidler. The front end of the donkey is Bill Mills with Vic Eades 'bringing up the rear'!

The 'Solva Shoot' gathered outside the Farmers Arms at Mathry before lunch in 1963. From the left are: David Harries, Willie Lamb, Michael Rodway, Douglas Baker, Roderick Willis, Bobbie Howell (partially obscured), Tom Pratt, David Ll. Roberts, Morgan Richards. In the 1920s and '30s the 'shoot' was run by a syndicate from Monmouth and Willie Lamb's father, a dour Scotsman, was the gamekeeper. After the war it was restarted by Owen Daniel and Morgan Richards, two local farmers, but when Commander Henry Wright retired from the Royal Navy and bought Tan-yr-Allt in the village he took over the shoot as he had the accommodation. He subsequently sold to Commander Douglas Baker on his retirement who then carried on with the 'shoot'.

This interesting house called 'The Fort' overlooking the harbour was thought to be named after the Iron Age Fort on the opposite bank. It was built in 1921 by Henry Evans for Jack Palethorpe, of the well-known pork establishment, as a holiday home but he only spent one holiday here as the only water supply was from a well which is just below the road on the way into the property. It became the family home of Captain David Evans, who was Commodore of the Blue Funnel Line of Liverpool. The footpath to Pengraig passes below the house from where there are fine views of the harbour and St Brides Bay.

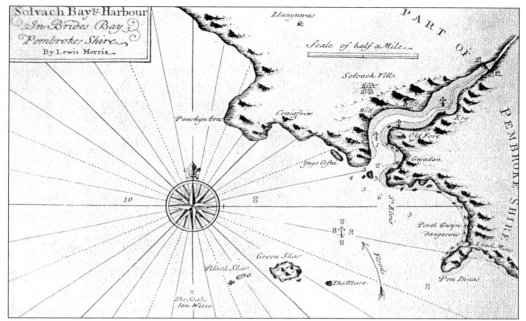

This chart by Lewis Morris, from 1784, shows the unique protection the bend in the harbour gives to shipping. Also the crosses below Pen Dinas that show some of the many wrecks that dotted the coastline. The word 'key' (south east of the estuary) is written where the lime kilns can now be seen; this was imported into Solva from the lime quarries of South Pembrokeshire, not only for the land, but also for building.

This is how the harbour would have looked at about the same time as the chart; the foundations of the hut on the lime kiln quay are still there. The two other quays are the Sand and Llanunwas quays. Two ships that were built on the foreshore at the beginning of the nineteenth century were the *Charlotte* and *Royal George* which were both over a 100 tons. The first record of sea trading was on 22 May 1602 when the *Guift* from Solva, with master John Richard, took a cargo to Waterford which included 3 qrs of Wheat and 3 qrs of Malt.

Steam to Solva, St. David's, &c.
NOTICE.

THE Directors of the Aberayron Steam Navigation Company—Limited—hereby give notice, that they intend to run their fast-sailing Screw Steamer, "PRINCE CADWGAN," A.A.1., between Solva and Bristol.

The Steamer will be taking in goods at Bristol July 5th and 6th, for Solva, St David's, Mathry, Castlemorris, Trevine, and Llandeloy, and places adjacent; and will continue to ply regularly between the above ports.

The support of the Merchants and Tradesmen of the above towns and neighbourhood is respectfully solicited.

The rate of freights will be the same as now charged to Haverfordwest.

For further particulars apply to Mr John Williams, Merchant, &c., Solva.

By Order,
WM. GRIFFITHS,
Secretary.

June 28th, 1869.

An advertisement in the local paper in 1869 announcing the first steam ship to run a service to Bristol. The *Prince Cadwgan* left Solva early on a dark morning in 1876, and struck a rock near Carreg Fran and sank off Porth Llisgi without loss of life. In 1894 the company acquired *The Norseman* which replaced *The Prince Cadwgan* and continued to trade with Bristol.

It was the custom of the time to construct a model of a boat to be built and this is the model of the *Solva Boat*. It was blowing a gale at the official launch, and to make himself heard the agent had to make his speech from the stern, then move to the bow and repeat it. There are four Trinity House Bodmin granite stones designating the boundary of the property which belonged to Trinity House around Solva Quay, and one can still be seen at the top of the slipway.

In 1869 it was decided to station a lifeboat on the quay which had been built by Trinity House in 1856 as a base for the new Smalls Lighthouse. As can be seen on the tablet on the side of the boathouse, it was funded by Mary Egerton as a memorial to her husband Capt. Charles Egerton, Royal Navy. In the following eighteen years the lifeboat was launched on service only four times, and due to the difficulties of launching at low water the station was closed in 1887. The boat was sold to a well-known member of the Mills family who was a fisherman out of Little Haven.

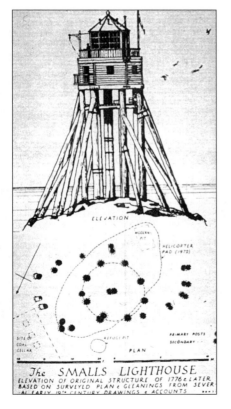

The SMALLS LIGHTHOUSE
ELEVATION OF ORIGINAL STRUCTURE OF 1776 & LATER.
BASED ON SURVEYED PLAN & GLEANINGS FROM SEVERAL EARLY 19TH CENTURY DRAWINGS & ACCOUNTS

In 1773 Cardigan-born John Phillips, a shipowner in Liverpool, was losing a number of ships, returning from the Far East and the Americas with valuable cargoes, on the reef known as the Hats and Barrels. He obtained a lease on the rocks and advertised in the local paper for someone to design an appropriate building which resulted in him accepting the design from musical instrument maker Henry Whiteside. In 1775 Whiteside arrived in Solva with his team which included eight miners. The weather was very bad that winter, so he pre-erected his design in the Gamlyn and decided that the cast iron supports would not 'give' in the Atlantic storms, and substituted oak beams; the iron stanchions that were not used can be seen at the entrance to the car park.

The cast iron stanchions were used as bollards on the 'new' quay that was built by Trinity House on which to construct the lighthouse. This replaced Whitside's 'barracoon' (a description from a later date) and the dressed stone masonry was carved for the lighthouse from some of the 3,696 tons of Bodmin granite that was brought by steam tug to Solva. The lighthouse has remained on the Smalls since 1861.

On the far side of the River Solfach is the Gamlyn, so called because it was where on a Sunday the lads of the village would play such games as 'pitch and toss' and gamble. It was here in the winter of 1775 that Whiteside built his lighthouse and the country folk from miles around flocked to admire his work. One young girl, a farmer's daughter from Llandruidion, on seeing herself in the reflector was heard to remark, 'people will say that George Rees has one daughter, let them come here and see that he has many. I am beside myself with the beauty of my sisters'.

This postcard of Solva quay in the early part of the nineteenth century was reproduced for the Prance family who ran the post office. The iron stanchions from the old lighthouse can be seen as well as the loading ramp. The hut adjacent to the *Durham* (right), at the top of the footpath from the quay was where the lifeboat rockets were stored. *The Norseman* is alongside with one of the Devon fishing boats astern. The weighbridge hut is long gone but the well is the same now as it was then.

The barque *Cashier* left Cardiff on the 6 February 1900 bound for the cape with a cargo of coal and eight passengers. Off Lands End she met a violent storm and was unable to make Falmouth and was driven north eventually into St Bride's Bay and anchored off Nolton. The storm increased and the anchors started to drag, the rigging was cut away to no avail. Answering a distress signal at 1700hrs on 16 February the Little Haven lifeboat put to sea and rescued the passengers and some of the crew, the captain and the sailing master stayed on board. A steam tug put out from Milford and after much trouble the ship was brought into Solva.

This postcard shows the timbers of the wreck of the *Cashier* stacked up outside Harbour House. Timbers from this wreck, and many others, can also be seen in a number of the older houses and cottages in the district. These houses were built with timbers from ship wrecks on the coast, and can be distinguished by the presence of 'treenails' in the beams and woodwork.

The motor barge *Harparees* can be seen alongside the quay, *c.* 1925. She was a 94ft wooden vessel built at a boatyard in Sittingbourne, Kent, in 1920 and was owned by three men, Messrs Harries, Parry and Rees of Newquay, Ceredigion. They purchased it to compete with the existing coastal trade on the west coast of Wales. In 1923, during the hard years of the depression, it was repossessed by the bank, to be bought again by Captain Parry who sold her in 1928. The new owner took her to the Isle of Wight, only to sink her off Calais in 1929, although thankfully without loss of life.

44

One vessel that did manage to trade successfully through the depression of the 1930s was the *Ben Rein* owned by Captain George of Trefin, seen here 'steaming' up the River Teifi towards Cardigan. She was built in Paisley for R.&W. Paul of Ipswich as the *Tern*, to be resold to the Ramsey Steamship Co. and renamed the *Ben Rein*. Captain George bought her in 1921 and she traded on the west coast until 1936 when she was sold to the Ilfracombe Coal and Salvage Ltd. On the 17 February 1941 she struck a mine $3\frac{1}{2}$ miles east of the Manacles on a voyage from Plymouth to Falmouth when two out of the crew of seven were lost (from *Cambrian Coasters*).

The *Staffa*, owned by the Eynon family of Angle, is seen unloading a cargo of coal. It was not unusual to see a line of horses and carts following the ebb tide, to start unloading as soon as they could. It was hard work shovelling the coal into the basket as they were not working on a 'flat floor'. The baskets were hoisted out of the hold by the boom, and emptied into the cart. There were a number of people in the village with the name Harry Davies and one of the men engaged for this work was known as Harry 'Discharge' (inset). There is a low wall on Solva quay, and the story is told of how Harry was taking a load of corn to be loaded on a ketch alongside, he said 'back, back' to the horse and finished up in the ship's hold! That is why the low wall was built.

The other ketch that was a regular visitor to the shores of Solva was the *Agnes*, with Captain Mitchell from Braunton in Devon. Leaving the Gaseg on the port side she is 'steaming' towards the harbour. On a quiet windless day her paraffin auxiliary engine could be heard across St Brides Bay as she approached from Jack Sound. Captain Mitchell's brother was the mate of the *Democrat* when, in 1910, the St David's lifeboat came to grief on the Bitches after taking off the crew in Ramsey Sound during a northerly gale.

The ketch *Annie* is seen alongside the quay in 1935. In the foreground is William Henry Davies from St David's. During the war he was in the Merchant Service, and died as a result of enemy action in one of the Atlantic convoys in 1941.

SA.24F.   Harbour and Village. Solva.

Shipping continued to trade from Solva until the outbreak of the war in 1939. The ketch *Annie* was well known on the west coast and regularly brought coal into the harbour. The owner was Captain William Jenkins who lived with his family in Gribin Cottage. The *Annie* was lost during the war in Milford Haven carrying sand from Angle.

Alongside the quay in 1939 was the South Wales Sea Fisheries patrol vessel *Feather*. The Chief Fisheries Officer was ex-submariner Lieutenant Commander Kirkpatrick-Crockett, Royal Navy (Rtd). On the outbreak of war, *Feather* was recalled to Swansea to be fitted out for wartime. On her return we found that she had been given a .303 rifle – and a bayonet!

47

A view of *Norseman* alongside the quay when the Annual Regatta was taking place in 1908. The event started as a competition between local farmers together with the boys of the village against the visiting seafarers; it was also recognized as an unofficial public holiday where the farmers would engage their labour for the next twelve months.

The finish of the four-oared rowing race with Tom Jewel of Appledore, captain of the ketch *Dolphin* built in Jersey in 1862, acting as committee boat. A young boy from the village joined the crew and, in 1932, became one of the youngest captains to have command of a tanker his name was Captain Benjamin G. Protheroe. The boat alongside the quay was owned by Captain Bill Brinham from Padstow who with the two boats fished between Solva and Fishguard in the early part of this century. The sailing boat astern of *Dolphin* is the *Redwing* owned by headmaster W.D. Evans.

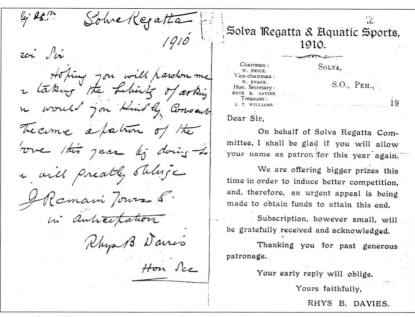

Raising money for village events is as much a problem today as it was in the 'good old days'.

In 1938 the committee decided to celebrate fifty years of regattas in Solva Harbour with a dinner in the Memorial Hall. Fifty years later a similar, centenary, function was held and these are copies of the original menu covers where similar fare was served. In 1938 the food was prepared and served by Nellie Pearce and staff of the Cambrian Hotel. The centenary dinner was prepared and served by Margaret Canby-Lewis and her staff of the Harbour House Hotel.

In 1934 the officials and friends were aboard the committee boat, *Feather*, which was anchored in the centre of the harbour. In the back row are visitors and in the middle row, left to right, are the skipper of *Feather*, Morris Lewis, Owen Thomas the county architect, Dr Saunders, Captain Beer from St David's who started the races, Robert Wheatley, Jim Price. In the front row are: Frank Angel of Cardiff, George Raggett, Dr Parry, Hendrick Howell the managing director of James Williams, cathedral organist Dr Joseph Soar, Lady Ramsden. In the front is W.H. John JP of the Guardian Office.

It was a fine day with a good crowd for the 1934 Regatta and the motor boat race is about to finish, with *Wattaw* owned by Walters, Adams and Thomas in the lead. The stern of committee boat *Feather* can just be seen on the right. The black launch on the left is owned by the Milford Docks Company, and next to it is the white painted *Gemini*. Bottom right is Peter Lewis's *Shushima*, and just above is Morris Lewis's *Viola* alongside the *Smiling Morn*. A cluster of boats are around the Brynach and just to the right, standing on the *Saucy Sarah*, is her owner Mr Webb who was a dentist in Ystradgynlais.

The five boats at this sailing race in 1937 were, on the left: the *Dilys* (owned by Morris Lewis and sailed by visitors), the *Redwing* (initially owned by headmaster W.D. Evans and sailed by Tom Cartwright who, as Commander in Wartime M.T.B.'s, was awarded a DSC,) Paul Raggett and Gwyn Morris in *Vera*, Lister Holliwell in *Jenny* and Peter Lewis with Gwyn Thomas in *Sushima*. In the background is *Saucy Susan*, owned by Mr Webb, and the boat which was acting as start boat, astern of Brinley Davies' tripping boat *Brynach*.

This regatta photograph, from around 1960, shows the dramatic increase in sailing, brought on by the development of improved plywood which had been used to build Mosquitos, now available in kit form which considerably reduced the cost of owning a boat. In the background are four RNSA sailing dinghies owned by the Royal Navy at HMS *Goldcrest*, the Air Station at Brawdy.

SOLVA YACHT RACE, 1925

By 1925 the Annual Regatta was beginning to attract larger boats that had come from as far away as Swansea and Fishguard: to the left are the *Pamela*, *Nigger* and *Lettie*, the race being won by the *Nigger*. This photograph of the sailing race was taken from the Gribin at low water and shows the two rocks at the entrance to the harbour, St Elvis and Black Rock, with the two attendant smaller rocks known as the Irishmen. These all combine to calm the fury of the Atlantic gales and shelter the harbour. On the 7 July 1927 the *West Wales Guardian* reported that 'the Hon. Sec. Mr J. Jenkins is busy completing the arrangements for the forthcoming regatta to be held on 12 August 1927'. It was later reported that the sailing race was won by Wally King, the landlord of the Cambrian Hotel in a 14ft international dinghy.

In the 1970s the Russian threat was such that NATO created a 'secret' American base at Brawdy to monitor the undersea movement of 'enemy' submarines; a cable was laid from Aber Mawr, across St Brides Bay and into the Irish Sea. On the balcony, in 1979, are amongst others: Captain Arno Laux (United States Navy), Paul Raggett, Alun Edwards, American station engineer Bob Harrison, Dr John Ross and Regatta Commodore Wyndham Lewis.

On 9 December 1988 a dinner was held in the Memorial Hall to celebrate the Centenary of Solva Regatta. A superb meal was provided by Margaret Canby-Lewis and her staff from the Harbour House Hotel. All the committee were present: left to right, back row: Richard Morgan, Piers Beckett, Andy Robinson, Stanley Clifford, Norman Payne, Iain Tite. Front row, sitting: John Rees, Celia Taylor, Paul Raggett, Helen Phillips, Peter Lewis.

With improvements in road and rail travel and easier methods of bringing goods to Solva and surrounding farms the scene in the harbour was changing to pleasure boating and an important but small fishing industry. Here, on Regatta day in 1955, is an ex-Royal Naval cutter bought by Willie Phillips for conversion into a lobster fishing boat. Quite a crowd has collected to watch the regatta and lifeboat Skipper Watts Williams has the *Swn y mor* alongside the quay.

The *Dorothy Ann* after she had been converted. She was lost off Carreg Rhosson off Saint David's on 19 August 1977. Despite the fact that Willie could not swim he managed to scramble ashore on to the rock and was rescued by helicopter. His grandfather and father had been rescued from this area many years before!

Attending to a magneto in his workshop is Willie's father Harry 'Cafran', so called because he was born on a smallholding above Solva Valley, near Middle Mill called Carn y fran. Like his father before him, he knew the coast well; he fished in the *Janwell*, a well-known boat, as she had been used to fish the North Devon Coast under sail by the Crockford family.

At Willie Phillip's wedding, in 1973, the triumphal arch of lobster pots was held aloft by, left to right: his brother Jacky, Benja Howells, cousin and harbour master Sharky Phillips and his father Harry.

At 0838 on Thursday 1 June 1995, in the morning mist, two ships could be seen steaming along the south of St Brides Bay; they were Her Majesty's yacht *Britannia* and her escort HMS *Cardiff*. She is seen here passing inside *Green Scar*, shortly after Her Majesty has disembarked; the royal barge is seen entering the harbour escorted by the 'Solva Fleet'.

The royal barge about to come alongside the quay. Her Majesty had come to visit St David's to present 'Letters Patent', thus granting city status. Her Majesty was received by the Lord Lieutenant David Mansel Lewis, chairman of the Harbour Authority Iain Tite, harbour master Sharky Phillips, chairman Jane Pascoe and members of the Solva Community Council.

At 0915 Her Majesty came ashore onto the Queen's Steps which had been built specially for her visit. In a later conversation with the Crucifer Nick Watson at St David's Cathedral Her Majesty asked where he came from, 'Solva Ma'am', 'it's a very pretty place', she replied, 'and very nice to come ashore in a place like that; when we use *Britannia* in the British Isles we usually find ourselves alongside a dock somewhere'.

It was the decision of Commander Tony Mason, the naval liaison officer at Pembroke Dock, that Solva be the appropriate harbour for the Royal visit. Admittance to the quay had been reserved for the local residents only and Her Majesty can be seen on the Royal 'walkabout' talking to the well-known Solva residents Margaret Williams, Elfair Williams and Irene Waters.

The fishermen of Solva taken outside the Lifeboat House, in 1955, are, left to right: Gerald Phillips, Willie, alongside his father Harry Phillips, Idwal Chapman, Robin Jenkins, Mervyn Evans son of Captain David Evans of the Fort, Reeve Crampton, Viv Jenkins. In the background are the typical 'withy' lobster pots that were made out of locally grown willow.

Idwal Chapman, who fished the Skomer and Skokholm Islands in his boat *Mizpah*, is on the quay in 1957 are holding a lobster pot similar to the 'withy' pots. They are, however, now being made of wire covered with netting. Next to him is boatman Robin Jenkins who as a boy went to sea with Captain Jenkins in the *Annie*.

The quay, bottom left, seen around 1908, was in all probability built to export roadstone from the quarry at Middle Mill, to try and compete with Porthgain; the remains of the quay were still to be seen in the 1930s. How successful the quay was is not known, but ships would only be able to come alongside at spring tides. W.H. Evans of Harbour House noted: 'December 17 1910. High tide. Yard door, shed door, weigh bridge and coach house doors burst in. I had a 1lb salmon swimming in the coach house. The vessel *Thomas & Son* washed up almost on top of this quay'.

In the winter of 1939 there was a gale of considerable force and small craft were carried up the main street and deposited outside the Cambrian. The Cornish sloop *Smiling Morn* was lifted over the footbridge and can be seen in the river. The cabin cruiser *Gemini* (the white boat on the right of the postcard) was stranded at the top end of the Gamlyn field. W.H. Evans noted: 'January 15 1939. Terrible storm. 4.15a.m. waves smashing boats – deluging our house, smashing shed door'.

Captain H.G. Davies was one of the pupils mentioned in an article in the Canadian Pacific Steam Navigation Company's magazine *Sea Breezes* (No. 17, Vol. II, April 1921 at a price of tuppence!) The editor was surprised to hear of the achievements of a small school 'in a little seaside village of 400 inhabitants in far away Solva', and the nautical training given by headmaster W.D. Evans, not only in the classroom, but the practical seamanship in his sailing boat *Redwing*. His father-in-law had also worked for the company and had been Captain of the RMS *Oronsa*. Captain Davies is seen with his ship TSS *Ucali*. When Captain Davies retired from sea, he farmed at Caerforiog, a short way from Middle Mill. When standing for local council election his campaign slogan was 'tap water for Solva'. Captain Davies was elected by one vote and was presented with a spade with which he dug the first turf, when water was brought to Solva in 1938.

A postcard of Captain Davies' ship the SS *Jane Radcliffe*, dated 22 December 1905, with the postmark, Sharpness, Berkely, Glos. It was sent from Captain Osborne Thomas of Elsinore addressed to Miss E.M. Phillips, 14 Hartington Road, Garston, Liverpool, and reads: 'Sharpness, leaving tomorrow. I don't know where we are going from here. I will send you another card tomorrow'.

THE BLUE FUNNEL LINE

FIRST CLASS PASSENGERS ONLY.

OUND
THE
'ORLD
OURS.

TOUR
IN
SOUT
AFRIC

T.S.S. "NESTOR."

In 1926, another of Solva's master mariners was Captain David Evans who married Dilys Evans of Llanungar Farm, and lived at The Fort, overlooking the harbour. He worked for the famous Blue Funnel Line, of Liverpool. His ship was the 14,547-ton TSS *Nestor* and at the time the inclusive first class fare to South Africa was £13. Subsequently he became Commodore of the Line.

Three
Inland Hamlets

A visitor arriving at Middle Mill in the late 1920s.

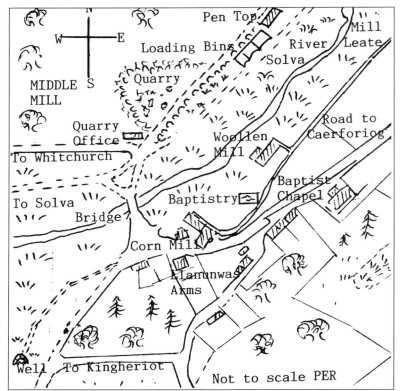

A mile upstream from Solva is the hamlet of Middle Mill and for its size it was very industrial, with a granite quarry, woollen and corn mills. There was also a public house called the Llanunwas Arms, just over the bridge, but it closed before the First World War. The corn mill ceased grinding corn in the early '50s. Felinganol Baptist chapel is situated on the side of the hill.

Felinganol Baptist chapel, seen 'sheltering' in the trees in Middle Mill in the 1930s, was erected in 1756 although services had been held on the site for ten years; the mother church was Llangloffan and the new Baptist church was incorporated in 1794. In the 1930s the pastor was the Revd Jubilee Young, whose powerful sermons were famous and some of them have been recorded. The quarry is out of the picture, but below the chapel alongside the river is the woollen mill and downstream is the miller's house, there is a millstone leaning against the wall. The traction engine to the left of the bridge worked in the quarry.

Middle Mill Quarry supplied much of the material for the construction of the roads of Pembrokeshire; it also provided work for the local farmers who were employed carting out the roadstone. The quarry was managed by Henry Evans who is seen below the crusher with the team in 1933. Left to right, back row: S. Bevan, G. Salmon, Percy Roberts, G. Williams, G. Miles, G. Davies, H. Phillips, G. Phillips, T. and G. Rees, G. Hughes, John Evans. Bottom row: Fred Mathias, Alf Beynon, D. Hughes, Harry Davies, G. Reynish, T. Howells, Henry Evans with six year old son John, G. Evans from Kingheriot. In October of that year G. Hughes was killed in a rock fall.

Just over the river Tom Griffiths is preparing and making up shuttles ready to start work.

The water wheel was repaired in 1950, but by 1960 it was beyond repair and was replaced by a Ruslyn Ackroyd $9\frac{1}{2}$ horsepower engine.

Before joining the Royal Air Force Eric Hemingway had been working in the woollen industry and specialized in dyeing the wool. Here he is with his father-in-law Tom Griffiths with the hanks of wool drying on the lines. In the background are the loading bins for the roadstone from the quarry.

Tom Griffiths sorting out the wool fleeces with the hand mule in the background.

The woollen mill was built by Thomas Griffiths and his family in 1907. It was originally driven by a water wheel and water can be seen 'cascading' over the wheel to the left in 1946. The water was carried to the mill by a man-made ditch, called a leat, which was connected to the Afon Solfach further up the valley. The leat was originally constructed for the use of the corn mill, and only later was adopted by the woollen mill as a power source; however this meant that both of the mills relied on it. Due to a number of 'dry' years, and to the fact that the wheel began to require a significant amount of restoration, a paraffin engine was bought for £10. When this was replaced by electrical power, the engine was sold as 'scrap', for £14! Thomas Griffiths retired in 1950.

This drawing by Campbell Cooper, from 1934, shows Thomas Griffiths at work on a hand loom that he himself built. He made the first woollen carpet in Wales which was sold to Lord Ramsden who had a house near Whitesands, St David's.

One of Tom Griffiths' regular customers was George John of Portland Square, Solva. He is seen, around 1940, inspecting the tweed for his next suit, which was to be made up by one of the local tailors. He was also a keen local fisherman and could often be seen fishing on the river. It was reported in the *Daily Express*, on the 29 June 1929, that the wool from Welsh Black Mountain sheep was 'sent to Griffiths' Mill at Solva in Pembrokeshire, where it was made into dark brown undyed cloth. The cloth was then sent to the Prime Minister, the Rt Hon. J. Ramsey MacDonald MP, and ever since [he] has had all his clothes made from the same material. "My favourite suit – a piece of Wales", was the Premier's comment, when questioned on the matter'.

Another view of the woollen mill with Tom Griffiths standing by the entrance door with a visitor in the 1950s. The 'sign' on the roof, 'Griffiths & Sons Woollen Mill', was painted by his son in law, Eric Hemingway, who had now joined him in the business. As can be seen the River Solva was in full flood.

Eric Hemingway was a radio operator/mechanic in the Royal Air Force, who was stationed at St David's airfield in 1943. He met Betty Griffiths and became engaged. When they were married they settled in Solva and he joined the family business. Here he is working on the new plant that was installed in 1962.

Betty Hemingway, serving a customer in the stockroom in 1975. The picture shows the interesting range of patterns that they were producing at the time.

An indenture, dated 1883, between the Ecclesiastical Commission and Henry Griffiths of Middle Mill, showed that he paid £96 for the mill house described as 'The Water Grist Mill and messuage or dwelling house, stables, kiln room, gardens, yard and offices'. The last man to work the mill was Clement Howell, in 1954, with his widowed niece Mrs Lloyd whose husband had been St David's watchmaker. They also kept a few cows, and he was referred to as 'the farmer' by poet, Doris Burge.

As a schoolboy, in 1983, James King (now an architect) researched a project on the mill, which his family owned, and these are the resulting photographs. He had first prize in a Civic Pride Competition, which had been organized by the *Western Mail*, the Welsh National Newspaper.

The corn to be ground was taken in through a door on the side of the hill.

After the corn was emptied into the receiving bins it dropped down onto the millstones, the flow would be controlled by the miller who would be below watching the meal flow into the bags.

Up the hill from Middle Mill, past the quarry is the hamlet of Caerfarchell. Looking across the common, in the 1930s, there was the shop kept by Maggie Gronow and in the adjoining building her brother, Hedley, had a workshop – he was one of the tailors of the district. Just above are the windows and roof of the Methodist chapel. The building to the right of centre was the communal well where there is now a telephone kiosk. The well was covered over in 1938 by Leslie Thorne and his father when mains water was laid on.

Hedley Gronow, seen on holiday in Trefin in 1952, was a 'mine' of information and always knew what 'went on' in the district. He had two mirrors set up in his workshop so that he could always see who was passing. His imitations of local characters were well known, a good example being his impersonation of the secretary of Solva Regatta Committee (who was also the local blacksmith) whose cap at the start of Regatta Day was 'fore and aft', and by 'stop tap' was 'athwartships'!

The small farming community of Skyfog close to Caerforiog Mill, not only had a blacksmith but also one of the last clogmakers in the district, Thomas James. He used sycamore wood, which grows well in Pembrokeshire, to make clogs in his workshop, a small green corrugated iron shed which is still standing. Thomas James was born in 1886 and in 1900 was apprenticed to John Morris Carpenter of Treffynon. In 1908 he set up as a clogmaker in Croesgoch. When he married in 1910 he moved to Skyfog where he continued his work and was very well known throughout the district.

In the hamlet of Trelerwr, situated on the coast halfway between Solva and St David's, was a small thatched church, where the bell was rung calling the children to Sunday school, it could be heard clearly in St David's when, in 1916, the last service was held.

A Halifax bomber being refuelled at St David's airfield, a mile north west of Solva in 1943. The airfield was constructed in 1942 and a temporary camp was also built, by Messrs Wimpey, for the many Irish labourers who came over to carry out the work. It was the most westerly airfield in Wales, and the first inhabitants were the United States Navy who were equipped with PB4Y Liberators and Halifax bombers. In September 1943 the unit was transferred to Dunkswell in Devon, and the RAF Coastal Command moved in.

The crew of a Halifax bomber in 1944. Fortresses from 206 and 220 Squadrons were the first aircraft to arrive at the airfield. However, these were replaced on 11 December 1943 by two Halifax from 58 Squadron and two from 502 Squadron; they were soon to be joined by the rest of the squadron. The squadron was very involved in the operations of the Second World War and during January 1944 their aircraft sighted ten U-boats at night, attacking nine, although with no observed results. Retaliation came in February when a JU88 destroyed a returning Halifax over St Brides Bay: only a wheel was recovered. The crew were, left to right, back row: Bill Fairhurst, Wilf Thornley, Eric Hemingway, ? Henderson (engineer). Front row: Freddie Hill, Bill Cohen (navigator), 'Skipper' Hannah (pilot), Rick Farmer. Eric Hemingway subsequently married Betty Griffiths of the Woollen Mill, which they eventually ran together (see p. 67-8)

The end of the road for Halifax No. HX 177. On returning from a mission over the Atlantic this Halifax No. HX 177 of 58 Squadron was coming into land on 20 July 1944, when the undercarriage collapsed and the aircraft veered into the control tower; it was a 'write-off' but the control tower remained standing – the crew walked away.

A large crowd at the Airwork Christmas party in their Mess, *c.* 1958. Seated and on the left is the chief engineer Bill Strawson and in the centre is the manager 'Tommy' Tompkins.

The ground crew of Airwork in front of one of the aircraft, *c.* 1968. They are left to right, back row: Alun James (armourer), Byron Davies (airframe fitter), Glyn Phillips (engine fitter), Brian John (engine fitter), Bill Lawrence (engine fitter), Aubrey Williams (radio engineer), Tony South (airframe fitter), Ken Jenkins (airframe fitter). Front row, seated: Bill Lewis (storeman), Huw Hannan (electrical fitter), Graham Beer (foreman), Ken Edwards (chief engineer), -?- (his secretary), Arthur Vickers (foreman), Jock Taylor (airframe fitter), Richard Evans (maintenance control).

The ground staff and pilots at St David's airfield in 1968. Initially Messrs Airwork operated from RAF Brawdy carrying out twin engine conversion courses for Royal Navy Pilots, but when training demands increased they were moved to St David's airfield. Included are, back row: ? Strawson (engineer), Jock Flynn, Spencer Phillips, Mike Carter, Dennis Farndon, Ken Edwards, 'Plimsol' Plimston, Dan Carter, Bill Slade, Dave Woodhead, Tam Aldous, Alun James, Joe Pugh, Bill Lawrence, Hopkin Evans, Ron Poole. Front row: John Harries, Wyn Richards, Denzil Thomas, Elwyn Davies, Ken Jenkins, Graham Beer, Brian John, Freddie John, Les Cartwright, Byron Davies, Jock Taylor.

Sea Venoms lines up in front of the control tower. There were three hangers, two of which can be seen in the photograph. Just above the sixth Venom from the right is the water tower, on the road to Solva, which serviced the airfield.

St David's airfield looking towards the city in 1947. The main problem when operating from the airfield (witnessed here) was the westerly runway, as the bombers could not take off with a full load because the Carn Llidi rock was in the way. In the 1950s these hangars were full up with Green Godesses, the wartime fire engines.

The control tower in its final throes with Carn Llidi, which is above Whitesands beach, in the distance, to the left. With the departure of Messrs Airwork a number of the buildings were beginning to get vandalized, in the interest of safety the Royal Navy decided to demolish the control tower.

The Royal Navy disposal team from Brawdy certainly did a tidy job. The National Park with the Aid of the Welsh Development Agency and a Eurogrant are at present endeavouring to restore the land to its natural habitat where plover once nested and merlin flew.

At the beginning of the nineteenth century the water for St David's came from Nawr Ffynon. The water was pumped up to the reservoir at the top of the hill which is still there. Down the valley at Porth y rhaw are the remains of a corn and woollen mill, which was once owned and occupied by the George family, including grandparents, parents and the three daughters who lived in the cottage on the left. The mills ceased to operate in 1915. In the background are the remains of an Iron Age promontary fort. In a recent excavation by Peter Crane of the Dyfed Archeological Trust, funded by CADW, the remains of at least nine dwellings have been unearthed and are said to date well into the Roman period (c. 150/175 AD).

The ruins of a grist mill at Caerbwdy, where George Harries of St David's, now in his nineties, worked as a boy. Just above the mill is a lime kiln and these are to be found on most of the bays and beaches on the west coast. They are usually round, but this one is rectangular, like the one on Skomer Island and a few of the others.

Workmen on the cliffs at Caerbwdy, extracting the hard red sandstone used to build the cathedral in St David's. In recent years considerable restoration to the fabric has been required.

Four
From Caerfai to Saint Justinian

'Manby's mortar device, used for firing lines to ships that were in distress. This was the equipment held by the Board of Trade's "Life Saving Apparatus" store in St David's. By 1823 Manby's apparatus had saved 229 lives.' (From *The Times*, 24 Wednesday November 1965)

Caerfai Farm, on the way down to the beach of the same name in 1882. Here is David Edwards with his pony Bob, his two daughters Elizabeth and Mary and his wife standing in the doorway of the farm.

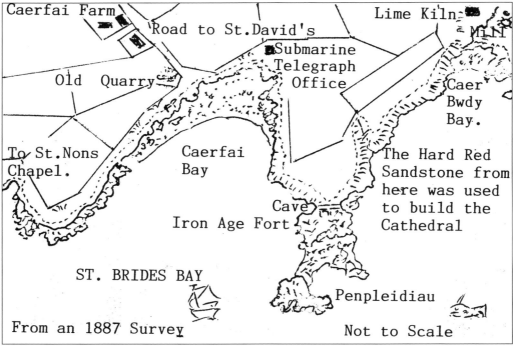

Caerfai Bay which was, at the time, the most popular bathing beach of St David's. In the 1930s there was a sign painted on the side of the cliff 'Ladies to the right – Gentlemen to the left'. On the promontory of Penpleidiau are the remains of one of the many Iron Age Forts to be found on the coast of St Brides Bay.

In 1856 Trinity House decided to replace Henry Whiteside's lighthouse with something more substantial. In 1896 the GPO laid a submarine cable to the Smalls so that lighthouse keepers could report the return of shipping to the head coastguard who would contact the Lloyds Agent in Liverpool. In this photograph you can see above the beach at Caerfai the hut where the cable terminated on the left. However, with improved sea to shore communications, the service was discontinued in 1927.

"The Smalls" Lighthouse.

Weather conditions had to be suitable for the relief of the lighthouse on the Smalls because of the exposed nature of the site; very much later helicopter pads were built to ease the change over. Today most of the lighthouses are automated and only require periodic maintenance. The inset is a commemorative stamp produced by the Post Office in 1998 featuring lighthouses and this one shows the helipad to enable maintenance to be carried out after they were all 'automated'.

The St David's 'Life Saving Apparatus' team outside their headquarters in 1909. These were the volunteer coastguards who were called out to assist in lifesaving. Sitting in the cart that carried the equipment out to the casualty, left to right: Ivor Arnold, J. Lewis, George Calder. Standing in front of the cart: ? Pomeroy, ? Bartholemew, ? Lewis (the tailor). The building is now the post office.

One of the last LSA carts which was used in Ireland. In 1988 the Fishguard station officer, Gwynfor John, was asked to collect this cart from Fishguard harbour.

The layout in the LSA carts. This was standard throughout the country and the exercise would be carried out time and again on practice nights as it was most important that the lines went out without 'snagging'. The correct drill appeared in the official booklet issued by the Board of Trade, published in 1913, and was entitled *Instructions relating to the Rocket Apparatus for Saving Life at Shipwreck*.

Included in the equipment on this cart was a small bag of coins which were given out by the coastguard in charge when the team were called out to a wreck. Later on the members of the team would present themselves at the station where the coin would be handed in and they would be suitably rewarded.

A print entitled 'The Loss of His Majesty's Steam Packet *Meteor* in 1830 off Portland' which shows lives being saved with the use of the mortar. A report in a local paper read 'that on the morning of the 17th October 1862, one of the Walters of St Elvis wended his way to the top of the cliff [and] on the identical rock on which the Victoria of Youghal was lost, he saw six men – not a vestage of a vessel was seen. The fact was reported to Captain John Rees of Mynydd Ddu, who brought over Manby's Mortar Apparatus. Several shots were fired without success – one more ball was brought over by Thomas Higgon of Tremaenhir, this took the line right over the rock. The five men and a boy were brought ashore and well looked after at the Cambrian Hotel. The ship was the *Oak of Belfast*'.

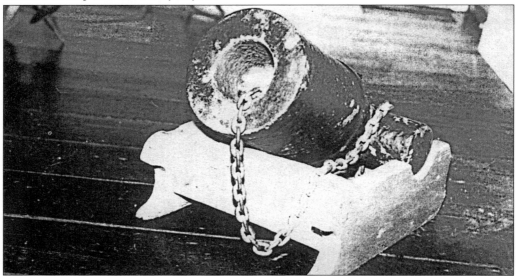

As can be seen the Manby Mortar was a very considerable piece of artillery and it could not have been an easy job getting it to where it was needed. Its creator, George William Manby was born in 1765 and became a captain in the Cambridge Militia. As the result of a visit in 1801 he published *The History and Antiquities of St David's*. A volume entitled *Captain Manby's Apparatus 1810 to 1820* is preserved among the ordnance papers in the Public Record Office. He died in 1854 after many years investigating the saving of life at sea. His mortar was replaced later in the nineteenth century by the Boxer Rocket.

The first coastguard station was on the rocky hill Carn Llidi at the end of the Peninsula, 181 metres above the beach at Whitesands. The coastguard service has been a part of the scene in St David's since the early part of the nineteenth century and this station was an integral part. In 1943, when there was an American base at St David's, one of their Marauder aircraft failed to clear the rock and crashed just below the summit killing the crew who all came from Virginia; thereafter the Americans called it Virginia Rock.

The original lookout, which was initially just below the top of the rock. It was presumably moved to a lower position because of low cloud and fog. In 1883 it was moved once again to Bryn y garn which is a rock adjacent to the Warpool Court hotel which gave it a commanding view of St Brides Bay.

The new station north of St David's Head near Porth Llong. It was 'manned' in 1956 and had superb views across Cardigan Bay; on a very clear days the distant Wicklow Hills. With no connection with mains electricity, the men had to rely on a generator to supply power for the radio, and food was cooked on Calor Gas which had to 'humped' manually over the rough track. The duty watch would leave their motorcycles at Porth Mawr farm and walk the mile to the station. In later years a new policy was adopted by the service and the coastal lookouts were withdrawn and 'watch' was kept on radio. The station closed in 1976.

A view above Caerfai Bay taken on a visit by senior staff from headquarters in 1973. This was probably one of the last with full time members. The five local members flanked by the two senior staff are, left to right: District Officer Robert Lewis, Auxiliary Coastguard Aaron Foster, Dr George Middleton, Station Officer William Williams and Coastguard Gwlym Davies.

The old lookout, outside the City Hotel. At the beginning of the twentieth century the lookout was pensioned off and placed outside the City Hotel for the sale of ice cream, where it remained until well into the 1930s.

Left to right: Jennifer Rees, Susan Roberts and Robert Rees, playing in the vacant lookout building on Rhosson Rock after yet another move in 1957. With the building of the lifeboat house and slipway at St Justinian it was decided that it would also be useful to build a lookout on Rhosson Rock, as it was now part of the coastguard's work to fire the maroons when instructed by the secretary. Dr George Middleton, in his book on the Lifeboat Service, recalls, 'in 1903 a telescope was provided for the lookout on Rhosson Rock.'

Benjie Cass whitewashing the Flemish chimney of Rhosson Uchaf in 1929. Rhosson Uchaf, which at this time was farmed by the Morgan family, lies below the lookout building. There are descriptions of similar farmhouses in Pembrokeshire in *The Welsh House*, by Doctor Iorwerth Peate, who was responsible for creating the Folk Museum of Welsh Life at St Fagans. The archaeologist and historian Richard Fenton was born in Rhosson, in 1747, and his *Historical Tour Through Pembrokeshire* was published in 1811.

Augusta, the first lifeboat which came to St David's in 1869. This 32ft sailing and ten oared pulling boat was donated by the Earl of Dartmouth and named after his wife. Initially the boat was stored in the yard of the Old Cross hotel and to haul her out, a 'bight' was taken round the lower part of the Cross, the marks can be seen today. Subsequently she was moved to Porthlysgi, where the Coxswain, David Hicks farmed. The boat was kept in a temporary boathouse in a small inlet on the north side of Porthlysgi Bay. In 1885, *Augusta* was replaced by the *Gem* a twelve oared rowing and sailing boat. The *Gem* was paid for by John Metcalf of York and was launched at the new boat house and slipway at St Justinian, an inlet on Ramsey Sound. Coxswain Hicks was still in command and was replaced by Thomas Davies in 1892, William Narbett in 1903, and by John Stephens in 1904.

In 1908 the coastal cargo steamer *Scotsman* was taking a short cut through Ramsey Sound when it is believed that she struck Shoe Rock. The captain managed to steer her into the cove at St Justinian and beach her alongside the lifeboat slipway; temporary repairs were made and she was able to continue on her way.

The RNLI lifeboat *Gem* with all sails set and crew aboard for her official launch, *c.* 1885. Twenty-five years later tragedy enveloped the *Gem* lifeboat. In a strong 'nor'westerly' gale at 10.30p.m. on the night of 12 October 1910, Captain Welsh in the ketch *Democrat* (who knew the Pembrokeshire coast well) decided to take shelter in the Watering, on the island side of Ramsey Sound. The wind shifted and the anchor started to drag, Captain Welsh had no alternative but to call for assistance. His signals were seen from the shore and the lifeboat was launched; they managed to come alongside the *Democrat* and take off the crew, but the fury of the storm together with the tide carried them towards the Bitches. Coxswain Stephens tried to steer the boat between the rocks, but she struck. Most of the crew managed to scramble on to the rock. The following day local men put out in a boat from Porthlysgi and were able to recover five of the survivors from the rock. What the survivors went through during the long night on that godforsaken rock, soaking wet and cold, beggars belief. The Coxswain John Stephens and crew members Henry Rowlands and James Price were swept away by the tide and the bodies were recovered the following day. It was Treginnis farmer William Thomas who managed to set his oilskins alight which drew attention to their plight.

Sam Husk, Sidney Mortimer and Sam Guppy, who met King George and were awarded the RNLI Silver Medal for their participation in the rescue from the *Gem*. Most of the publicity for the rescue went to the first boat that reached the Bitches and these men who brought off five of the survivors. Eleazer James also set out in his boat with John Davies, Adrian Arnold, another John Davies and Ivor Arnold and were awarded five gold sovereigns. Sidney Mortimer took over the replacement lifeboat, but a year later, on the arrival of the first motor lifeboat the *General Farrel*, Mortimer was replaced by Ivor Arnold.

The survivors of the Gem seated under the Old Cross. Left to right, back row: William Thomas from Treginnis, Thomas Evans 'Twm Quick', Sidney Mortimer, James Thomas from Rhodiad, Francis Rowlands from Pencnwc. Front row: William Banner, -?-, Willie Parry of Treveiddan House, the Second Coxswain George Martin, Captain Welsh of the *Democrat*, carpenter James Williams of Beehive House, the mate Mitchell of the *Democrat*, Michael Moriarty. Mate Mitchell's brother was Captain Mitchell of the *Agnes*, another ketch that was a frequent visitor. The irony of this disaster was that the *Democrat* remained afloat throughout and was anchored in the Watering.

With the loss of the *Gem*, it was decided that she should be replaced with a motor lifeboat, to be called the *General Farrell*, and a new boathouse and slipway. In the meantime a temporary rowing/sailing boat *Charlotte* was kept at Porthclais. The official launch of the *General Farrell* was in July 1913 with Coxswain Ivor Arnold at the helm. The coastguard lookout had been moved to Rhosson Rock, above the boathouse which gave better communication between the two services. After twenty-five years service at St David's the *General Farrell* left for another station. She was replaced by the more powerful and up to date petrol driven boat named *Swn-Y-Mor* (meaning Sound of the Sea).

Swn-Y-Mor being hauled up into the boathouse in 1936. She was a gift from the Civil Service and her new Coxswain was 'Cape Horner', Captain Williams Watts Williams (inset). Many rescues were carried out in wartime but, because of strict security, received no publicity. The many adventures of the St David's lifeboats have been related in the book on the lifeboats by Dr George Middleton, assisted by Desmond Hampson.

Captain Williams Watts Williams (who served on the *Howth*) was one of the many respected Master Mariners of the district and was proud of the fact that he served 'before the mast' and that he was also a 'Cape Horner'. He was Coxswain of the St David's lifeboat from 1936 to 1956 and one of his most remarkable achievements was also one of the biggest single rescues by a lifeboat. The twenty-thousand-ton tanker *World Concord* broke in half off the Pembrokeshire coast on 27 November 1954. The lifeboat was launched into a southerly gale with heavy rain squalls. When they arrived, the boarding ladder was hanging over the stern of the aft half of the ship, and the Coxswain asked for it to be moved forward, as the propeller was still threshing in the water. There were thirty-five survivors who were taken off one at a time and the operation lasted 50 minutes. The lifeboat was at sea for 7 hours and Coxswain Williams was awarded the RNLI Silver Medal for this remarkable achievement in atrocious conditions.

A practice run in Ramsey Sound with the lifeboat station astern in 1948. Included are: Emlyn John, Johnny Thomas, Gwyn Thomas, Dai Lewis the Mill, Howell Roberts, Willie Watkins, Coxswain Watts Williams, Jenkin Davies, Perkin Jones, Ossie Jones. Jenkin Davies (inset) and his brother Gwilym served on the lifeboat for many years and he also took trips round Ramsey Island; he was affectionately known as 'Captain Crunch'. His brother was on the lifeboat for the famous *World Concord* rescue – and later joined HM Coastguard.

A view of the *Swn-Y-Mor* on the slipway for an inspection by the RNLI taken by Studio Jon of Fishguard in 1952. Left to right, standing on the lifeboat: the Inspector, Engineer George Jordan, Coxswain Watts Williams, Bowman Dai Lewis. In front: Emlyn John, Howell Roberts, Dewi Rowlands, Billy Rowlands, Ken James, the Hon. Sec. Dr Joseph Soar, Ivor Grifiths, Jock Chisholm, Perkin Jones, Willie Morris, Ieuan Bateman.

Members and friends of the crew of the St David's lifeboat at a dinner at the Ship Inn, Solva in 1955. Left to right: seated at the table: the District Inspector of the RNLI, the Coxswain Captain W. Watts Williams, Hon. Sec. Dr Joseph Soar MBE, Engineer George Jordan and guest Col. Browning from St David's.

David Lewis (inset) who took over as Coxswain in 1956. After twenty years service to the Institution, Captain Williams retired and David Lewis replaced him. It was in the autumn of that year that the *Swn-y-Mor* was launched to go to the aid of a French trawler in distress off Skokholm. It successfully rescued eight crewmen, but sadly on entering Milford Haven they were engulfed by a huge wave and Ieuan Bateman was lost overboard; he was posthumously awarded two medals by the French Government. In 1963 the boat was replaced by the *Joseph Soar*, named after the Hon. Sec., after forty-one years service to the institution. Her Royal Highness Princess Marina was present for the launch on 19 May 1964.

The *Joseph Soar* rounding the South Bishop Rock lighthouse on a practice run.

Porth Clais, St David's. The man standing on the shore is probably the harbour pilot, Johnny Thomas, who lived in 'Halfway' a cottage on the way down to Porth Clais, as his longboat is on the left in Twll Pat. When he saw a vessel arriving in the cove he would row out and take one of the crew on board so they could start to tow the ship into the harbour. Meanwhile the two left on board would unship two long 'sweeps' and also start to row; this was before auxiliary engines were fitted. He would always moor the ships in the same place for unloading and the trench made by the keel (centre) is very clear.

The River Alun which rises inland at Llandigigi and flows down bisecting the cathedral from the Bishop's Palace to the narrow winding creek of Porth Clais, the harbour of St David's. It is said that stone from Caerbwdy, which was used to build the cathedral as well as Irish oak, for the roof of the nave, was landed here. Lime was also imported locally, through the harbour of St David's. It is recorded that this lime was, as early as 1324, imported to be used as a fertiliser and to make mortar for building and as a whitewash; the kilns have recently been restored by the National Trust. Here, five to six hundred years later, they are unloading lime from a sloop in the harbour. A horse and cart are emptying limestone into the kiln on the left. The building on the right was the Mariners public house which was licensed to Shemi Stune.

The gas works were built at the top end of the harbour, to supply the city, in 1901. However, when North Sea Gas was brought to St David's in the 1970s it was closed. To the north west was Capel y Pistyll and just below was a well, known as Ffynon Ddewi, which was said to have sprung miraculously for the patron saint, David, to be baptised by the Bishop of Munster.

The son of manager Bill Morris discharging the retorts, c. 1953. This was hard work and once started had to be finished. It required many hours 'all for a measly £3.00 per week', as described by the former chairman of Welsh Gas, Mervyn Jones, in his autobiography.

Five
St David's

The St David's branch of the Royal British Legion marching past the Cross to present their Colours to the cathedral on 11 November 1928.

The fourteenth-century High Cross standing in the centre of the old market square, where the four principal streets of the city meet. To quote George William Manby who wrote *The History and Antiquities of St David's* in 1801: 'formerly near the Cross stood the Market House, but no vestige remains. St David's has evidently been a place of considerable size and had two weekly markets, on Mondays and Thursdays, and was governed by a Mayor chosen annually'. By 1921 the Cross Square had taken on quite a military appearance with two cannons from the Crimean War.

THE OLD WINDMILL NOW TWR-Y-FELIN.

The old windmill, now Twr-y-felin. According to the *History of St David's* by Henry Evans, published in 1923, this was one of the three working windmills in the district. It was erected by George Llewellyn and his two sons in 1806 and suffered severe buffeting from the strong gales that occur on this exposed coast. There was one occasion when the 'sails' required attention and a gust of wind set the mill in motion with the miller still aboard, it went round three times before being stopped! The mill was bought by David Evans in 1861 and continued to grind corn until 1904 when the owner raised the tower and Felin Wynt became Twr-y-felin.

St David's Horse Show in 1916. By this time Twr-y-felin had become quite a feature of the landscape, and was by now established as a hotel. During the Second World War it was occupied by the Royal Navy as a base for Wrens who operated radar. At the end of hostilities it once more catered for visitors but in recent years it has become a well-known and popular activity centre.

NEUADD DINAS DEWI.
Agorwyd Tachwedd 3ydd, 1924.

ST. DAVIDS CITY HALL.
Opened November 3rd, 1924.

CHILDREN LAYING FOUNDATION STONE, 1920.

The late Capt. SAMUEL ROACH, St. Davids, who Died February 1st, 1919, bequeathed the sum of One Thousand Pounds towards the erection of these Buildings.—"He Loved His Native Place."

THE CITY HALL—Opened November 3rd, 1924.

MEMORIAL HALL & MUSEUM—Opened 1922.

The opening of the Memorial and City Halls.

Local school children holding copies of a leaflet produced for the opening of the Memorial Hall (seen on the previous page) which had taken place the previous year. They are outside the administrative centre of St David's, the City Hall, which was opened in 1924 by Mrs Blanche Roach of Cardiff, the sister in law of Captain Samuel Roach of Belmont. He had died on 1 February 1915 aged eighty-one and left £1,000 in his will for the building of the Memorial Hall.

Members of the parish council from 1952 to 1957. Left to right, back row: Brigadier Pim, J. Beynon, G. Lloyd, Dr Elliot. Middle row, staggered: R. Watkins, D. Howell, W.G. Llewellyn, D. Evans, D. Morgan, D. Morris, S. Mortimer, D. Jones, I. Martin, W. Mendus J. Thomas. Front row, seated: Chairman D. Nash and Vice Chairman G. Nash. Inset left is J. Salmon who died in August 1954 and was the chairman in May 1954.

The new council in 1958. Left to right, on the pavement at the front: H. Harries, Dr G. Middleton, J. Beynon, N. Hurley, Elliot Morris. On the first step: D. Evans, Miss C.M. Rees, J. Davies. At the back, staggered: Lloyd Harries, W. Jones, D.G. Morgan, D. Evans, J. Bateman, F. Jeffrey, D. Morgan, P. Davies, A. John.

The council chamber in 1966. Left to right, around the table: Jim Richards, R. James, Arthur John, James Wilcox, Robert Lloyd, 'Bunty' Price, John Edwards, Fred Jeffrey, Chairman D. Watts-Evans, Andrew Gray, William Llewellyn, Jenkin Davies, Dorothy Walters, Pamela Williams, D.G. Morgan, Dr George Middleton, Basil Williams.

A happy scene around the Old Cross celebrating the Jubilee of King George V in 1935. In front and to the right of the flag pole is the cathedral organist, Dr Joseph Soar. Many other characters were present including Willie Miles of Caerhys Farm, directly in front of the flag pole, Dai Lewis the mill behind the drum and little Valerie Howell in the foreground.

Her Majesty Queen Elizabeth II accompanied by His Royal Highness the Duke of Edinburgh paying their first visit to Saint David's Cathedral in 1953. It was the first time an English monarch had visited the cathedral since Henry II (1154-89).

Her Majesty and the Duke of Edinburgh pictured with the Rt Revd Bishop Havard and the Rt Revd Dean Whitton Davies in the Deanery garden after lunch.

Her Royal Highness, the Princess Royal Commandant of the Red Cross, who came to St David's to open the new Red Cross Centre in 1954. At the service in the cathedral are the two standard bearers, Hwyel Rees and Henry Griffiths. The taller boy in Red Cross uniform (centre left) in the choir stalls subsequently became Wing Commander Robert Williams OBE Royal Air Force. To the left of the hymn board is John Smith with Roy Watkins, David Wordley, Bill Morris (Coxswain of the lifeboat), and Canon Lloyd of Llanbadarn to the right.

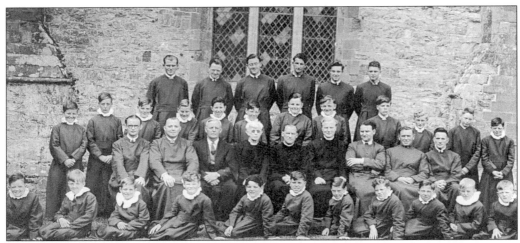

The choir outside St David's Cathedral in August 1955. Left to right, back row: John Davies, Donald Arnold, Roy Watkins, Basil Davies, Brian Devonald, David Thomas. Second row from the back, the boys of the choir: James Wilcox, Richard Wilcox, Owen Griffiths, Terry Roach, Austin Hooper, John Richards, Keith Thomas, John Hughes, Michael Davies, Raymond John, David Harries, Jock Hughes. Third row, seated: David Wordly, John Smith, the verger George Harries, Professor Harries from Lampeter, the Very Revd C. Whitton-Davies Dean of St David's, minor canon Cliff Williams, organist Peter Boorman, William Roberts, George Fox. Front row, seated on the ground: Dennis Price, Peter Whalton, Trevor Martin, Richard Jones, Adrian Boorman, Jim Lamb, Terry Williams, Peter Martin, ? Williams, David Morgan, Elmor Roberts.

Frank Lamb (left) and Jimmy Munroe (right) outside a disused grain warehouse on 13 February 1951. In 1946 Eric Taylor (inset) set up Otter Controls in Buxton. He had been coming on holiday to St David's for a number of years and would go out fishing with Frank Lamb. He liked the area so much that he bought Halfway, a cottage on the road to Porth Clais, and decided to expand his company to St David's. The disused grain warehouse at the bottom of Goat Street proved to be the perfect site (having previously been occupied by among other things a scout hut and fish and chip shop). He bought, renovated and occupied the building and it was named Twll Dwrgi.

Eric Taylor's business (centre right) supplied thermostats all over the world. Demand for thermostats increased and exports were made to Germany and even as far away as Japan. Many domestic appliance companies were supplied as well as a wide spectrum of motorcar manufacturers from Toyota to Rolls Royce! The factory had to be increased in size with an extension to the rear of the main building.

The staff outside Twll Dwrgi in 1957. Left to right: Muriel Davies, Betty Harries, Pat Reed, Marlene John, Ada Beer, Jean Hughes, Joan Roberts, Isabelle Davies, Eira Morris. Seated is Hilary Beer.

A GWR motor accident on Solva Hill, 13 December 1916. The Great Western Railway had inaugurated a bus service from Haverfordwest station to the City Hotel St David's in 1910, and the running of it had been smooth until 1916. It must have been quite an event when this solid tyred omnibus skidded on a patch of ice just above the quay road, and came to rest against the wall above the harbour. Fortunately the wall withstood the impact, otherwise the bus and passengers would have plunged down onto the rocks below. Only Mr Horton, the driver from St David's, sustained an injury, to his thumb. The children from the school just above, were marched down the hill to view the incident.

The Dewisland & Kemes Guardian
31st July 1869

Saint David's Omnibus.

THE ST. DAVID'S OMNIBUS leaves the MARINERs HOTEL, Haverfordwest, every Tuesday and Saturday afternoon, at Four o'clock, p.m.

LIST OF FARES:

		Inside.		Outside.	
		s.	D.	s.	D.
St David's to Haverfordwest	...2	6		2	0
Solva to Do.	...2	0		1	6
Penycwm to Do.	...1	3		1	0
Victoria t Do.	...1	0		1	0

W. WILLIAMS, Proprietor.

N.B.—Passengers are allowed to take 28lbs of luggage free of charge.

The St David's omnibus timetable from July 1869. City Businessman W. Williams, of the Cross Square, started the first regular connection to Haverfordwest and published the timetable in the weekly newspaper printed at the Guardian Office in Solva.

Drivers and conductors are seen at the opening of the new depot in December 1954. The first pneumatic tyred bus came into service in 1920, and this development heralded a dramatic increase in the speed of the buses – from 12 to 20 miles per hour! The St David's Omnibus company was taken over by Great Western and they in turn were bought by the Western Welsh Omnibus Company Ltd of Cardiff in 1929. As can be seen at the opening of the new depot in December 1954, the company provided employment for a considerable number of local people with eight buses on the road, and just after the war they were also running double deckers. In 1971 Western Welsh withdrew and Hugh Collins of Cuffern, Roch, carried on the service until 1973 when Marchwood Motors of Southampton came on to the scene. In 1981 Richards Brothers of Moylgrove arrived and are running the service to this day.

Left to right: Jack Thomas, Noel Thomas, Don Arnold, Ellis Davies, Les James (who had a taxi service in Haverfordwest) and Les Mathias at one of Western Welsh's annual dinners, in 1948, held at Warpool Court. The Western Welsh bus company were a 'sociable' organization and every year they had a dinner for their employees. It must be said that in pre-war days there was an hourly service and the buses would stop at all the pubs along the route and give a 'toot'!

Jacky Morgan, the well-known contractor from Pen y cwm, with his brother William of Perche Farm, 'at the helm', on their way with the threshing machine to Barch Farm, Camrose, in 1932. The traction engine was also used to carry roadstone from Middle Mill quarry, and can be seen on the left of the bridge near Middle Mill (see p. 62).

Left to right: Ceinwen, Martha and Leila the three daughters of William James of Tremynydd Farm in 1918. They are preparing to milk the cows with their 'mob' caps on their heads and carrying wood milking pails (which are called 'stwcs') and three legged milking stools.

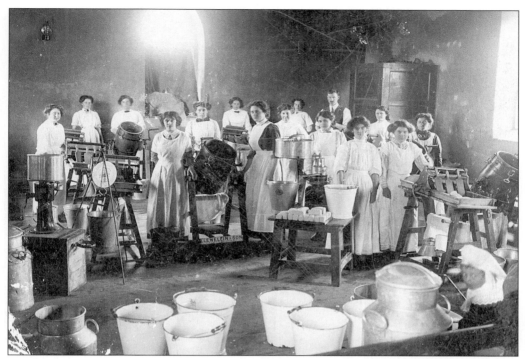

Local women attending a session in the Vestry of Taberbnacle chapel put on by G. Llewellin & Son, c. 1915. Ceinwen James remembers that at this time G. Llewellin & Son, of the Prize Churn Works in Haverfordwest, were touring the district giving instructions on the use of their equipment. Corn, butter and cheese were the main exports. These were not only shipped from the local harbours, but when the railway came, were delivered to Mathry Road station for delivery to Swansea, Cardiff and the towns of South Wales.

The cover of G. Llewellin & Son's complete illustrated dairy catalogue. G. Llewellin & Son were established in 1796, and won a considerable number of First Prizes, Gold and Silver Medals with their churns. It is interesting that in their advertisements it states that 'All Orders over £2 net, Carriage Paid'!

The committee at one of the annual ploughing matches at Trevacoon in 1955. They are, left to right, back row, staggered: George Davies, Owen Williams, Willie James, Neville Davies, John Griffiths (chairman), Willie James, Albert Evans, John James, Elwyn James, Mervyn Harries, William Williams, Perkin Jenkins, Willie Miles, Robert Thomas. Kneeling: Willie Davies, Vernon Hughes, Jim Morgan, Joe Davies, Willie Lloyd, Arthur John. The first official match took place on the 19 February 1924. This event was very important as it supported and celebrated the pastoral way of life. Agriculture played a most important role on the St David's Peninsula; however it was a land of no great depth or fertility, therefore there was a need to import lime from the south (the first recording on this was as early as the middle of the twelfth century). John Griffiths (fifth from the left, back row) was not only a champion ploughman but also a National judge, having attended matches in many areas. When young he accompanied his father Louis, in their horse and cart, down to the harbour, to unload and deliver coal from the ships around the district, as well as carrying out roadstone from the nearby quarry. He was also well known for his singing in local choirs.

Len Phillips of Solva competing in the St David's Ploughing Match at Brawdy Farm in 1987 where he won the Hydraulic Vintage Class Cup. The Preseli Hills in the background set the scene.

Haymaking at farmer/artist Herbert Oakley's Glasfryn Farm at St David's, *c*. 1930. Lifeboat hero Ivor Arnold (centre) eventually took over the farm, while his son became Captain S.R. 'Jim' Arnold of the Blue Funnel Fleet of Liverpool, and eventually a director of the line. Ivor Arnold's daughter, Rosina married Andrew Gray (inset) who continued to farm Glasfryn and became the first chairman of the Pembrokeshire Coast National Park in 1973.

Harvesting corn at Treginnis with a horse drawn reaper and binder in 1942. The men were, left to right: Hywel Roberts, Francis Rowlands, Jim Evans from Solva, Frank Waltham. The two children helping were evacuees from London. The hill of Carnllundain to the left of the horses head is on Ramsey Island.

Agricultural contractor Owen Rees threshing corn for farmer Perkin Jones in front of Treginnis farmhouse. On top of the ricks are, left to right: Tom Nicholas, Eric Carr and Perkin Jones with Edwin Phillips 'feeding' the machine. Standing between the drive belt from his Nuffield tractor is Owen Rees with Arthur John tying the sacks.

Perkin Jones combining corn at Treginnis Farm with his Ransome MST 42 Combine Harvester in the autumn of 1975. Two boys on holiday are sitting on the sacks of corn with, left to right: Ritchie Martin, Perkin Jones, Roy Thomas with his corgi, Dewi Rowlands, Jimmy Havard who lived in a cottage at Nine Wells.

Treginnis Isaf Farm, the most westerly farm on mainland Wales, situated on a Peninsula with Ramsey Sound on one side and St Brides Bay on the other. Because of its outstanding natural beauty, the farm was bought by the National Trust on the 8 May 1984. The area has a history of shipwrecks and copper mining with many interesting characters living there over the years. There is a small inlet to the west called Carn-ar-Wig where farmer Thomas would hoist out his lobster boat and which is reputed to be the place where the pilgrims embarked for Ramsey Island then inhabited by St Justinian and his followers.

A postcard of the farm drawn by 'Shoo' Rayner of the 'Mother' School in Devon. The National Trust used the farm for a time as their local base, but because of the range of buildings, which were unsuitable for modern mechanized farming methods it was decided to find an alternative use. By chance a Trust member heard that a 'Farm School' in Devon were looking for a farm in Wales, very soon it became a 'Farm for City Children'.

Her Royal Highness Princess Anne, patron of Farms for City Children, was at Treginnis on the 7 June 1991 to perform the official opening of the farm school. The founder Michael Morpurgo is on the extreme left, next to Her Royal Highness. Behind, with arms folded is the late Poet Laureate, Ted Hughes, who was a neighbour and friend to the Morpurgo's. They watch as farm director's son Andrew Plant presents a book to the Princess, with Clare Morpurgo (co-founder of the school) in the hat on the right. The school is a recognized part of the Educational Curriculum and classes come with their teachers: the pupils are divided into three sections, school work, domestic and farming.

Pupils in St David's County School in March 1938. Left to right, back row: N. Price, R. Bowen, P. Jenkins, J. Morris, E. Williams, B. Murrow, M. Jones, A. Evans, R. Price, D. Walters, D. Thomas, N. Charles, F. Harries, B. Lewis, B. Bevan, J. George, A. Evans, H. Thomas, I. Evans, I. Griffiths, H. Mortimer, P. Evans, A. James, P. Jenkins, M. Thomas, W. Davies, W. Beynon, S. Harries, T. James, H. Jones, R. Davies. Second row from the back: N. Martin, N. Phillips, J. Gwyther, E. Phillips, M. Miles, J. Jenkins, E. Beynon, M. Edwards, M. Smith, M. Jones, M. Evans, N. James, N. Rees, M. Evans, A. Evans, S. Harries, G. Walters, E. Williams, A. Morris,

The winners of the Welsh Schools Drama Cup at Llangefni in North Wales from St David's County School, c. 1948. The drama aspect of St David's County School was in the very capable hands of the Deputy Headmaster Islwyn Thomas. Left to right, back row: Islwyn Thomas, James Nicholas, Rees Jones, J.J. Evans (headmaster from 1936 to 1959). Front row, seated: Joyce Jenkins, Nita Evans, Nesta Roberts, Morffydd Harries, Elaine Evans.

P. Raggett, I. Price, J. Beynon, J. Jenkins, B. James, T. Harries, D. Bowie, D. Davies, I. Price. Third row: R. Thomas, S. Morris, E. Price, O. George, M. Lewis, B. Williams, M. Thomas, E. Tudor, Miss Jenkins, Miss Williams, Miss Davies MBE, Miss Rees, Mr J.J. Evans (headmaster), Mr Davies, Mr Jones, Mr Aspinal, Mr Thomas, A. Jones, C. George, R. Miles, B. Jenkins, M. Walters, L. Thomas, D. Davies. Front row, on the ground: P. Thomas, W. Lewis, D. Gronow, P. Evans, D. Davies, H. Page, R. Davies, L. Williams, T. Williams, D. Davies, D. Davies, I. Lewis, G. Phillips, H. Davies, J. Richards and R. Davies.

A performance of *Saint Joan*, which took place in Ysgol Dewi Saint on the 19, 20, and 21 December 1960. During his stay at St David's, Islwyn Thomas produced many plays in English and Welsh, and will be remembered most for his production of T.S. Elliot's *Murder in the Cathedral* which took place in St David's Cathedral. He is seen here (inset) with the production team and actors for *St Joan*.

St David's Rugby team in 1955/6. The team was re-started after a number of years and left to right, standing are: Alan Thomas, Joe Rees, Derek Davies, Jim Rees, Dai Narbett, Dewi Jenkins, Cyril Jones, Norman Broaders, Idris Morris. Centre: Tony Jones. Front row: Garrett Price, Norman Davies, Gerald Davies, I. Evans, Dai Richards.

St David's schoolmaster Odo Saunders, the
first president of the club, who had played
for the Welsh Secondary Schools against
France in 1926. Together with Dewi Jenkins
of Lloyds Bank (the first treasurer), Inspector
Winston Jones, Deputy Head of the local
secondary School Islwyn Thomas and Dai
Narbett of the City Hotel, Odo was
responsible for restarting the Rugby side in
1954.

The Rugby youth team in the 1973/4 season. Left to right, back row: G. Preece (fixture
secretary), W. Candler, R. Bateman, A. Williams, T. Evans, D. Bennett, T. Jenkins, N.
Cartwright, A. Whitfield, I. Hughes (youth team secretary). Front row: G. Price, R. Morris, P.
Sage, M. Walsh (captain), G. Carder, J. Rogers, R. Hughes.

Stanley Baldwin (president) presenting the 'Tom Jones' Cup to Martin Walsh who was the Youth Player of the Year in 1974. In the foreground is the Dean of St David's, The Very Reverend Bowen who in his youth had played rugby for Llanelli.

The Players Squad of 1978/9. They include, left to right, back row, staggered: J. Rogers, L. Owen, J. Bateman, T. Davies, M. Davies, M. Roberts, D. Jenkins, W. Candler, E. Joyce, S. Candler, R. Davies, A. Williams, G. Griffiths, D. Bennett, R. Jones, K. Jones, C. Evans, T. Rees, R. Collelo, D. Davies, I. Richards, J. Broaders. Front row: K. Phillips, B. Griffiths, R. Hughes, T. Jenkins, M. Walsh, G. Hughes, R. Bateman, J. James, N. Lewis.

Mrs Mildred Driver presenting the Driver Coronation Cup to D.G. Jones in 1937. Among those present were: Eva Walsh, Ruth James, M.L. Martin, Maggie Richards, Arthur Driver, M.L. Martin, Mrs Mendus, Mildrid Driver, Catherine Rees, Leslie Owen, D.G. Jones, I.O. Martin, M. Jones (Lloyds Bank), Mr Evans (Porthmawr), Morris Mendus and D.C. Evans. The four in the front: J.J. Jenkins (headmaster), Mr Jones (manager of the Midland Bank), Mr Davies (Gwynfryn), Gilbert Martin.

A receipt for the building of the clubhouse at Whitesands dated 24 April 1931. The golf links at Whitesands, the most westerly headland in Wales, were established in 1911, and the site has quite remarkable views of the coast. In 1930 the committee decided to build a 'proper' clubhouse, which was pre-fabricated at Hebden Bridge and delivered to Mathry Road Station to be erected by local contractors.

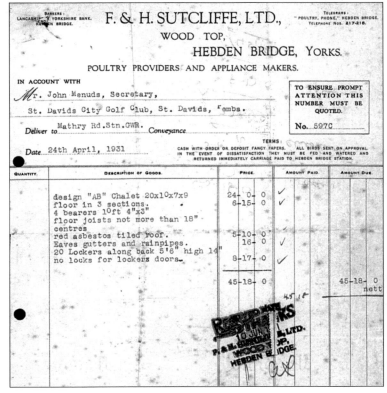

The Llanrhian Under 12 team at Narberth, in 1998, when they played in the Junior League Cup Final. It was the only game they lost that year. The team was, left to right, back row: A. Chambers, G. Evans, M. Parkin, B. Whitehead, P.Phillips. Front row: L. Jones, B. Jones, G. Morris (captain), C. Garrett, R. Devonald.

The Llanrhian Cricket Club initially played on a triangle of land adjacent to Manor Farm, Llanrhian. Due to the restricted area they had to play on, they were offered a field by one of their enthusiastic players, Farmer Elliot Morris, adjacent to his house, where it is now well established. In 1951 the club as reformed and in the 1st XI were: Perkin Jenkins, Herbert Roach, Gwilym Charles, Trevor Rees, Ronald Stephens, Gordon Cawood, Lesley Hooper, Ritchie James, Elliot Morris (captain), Kenvyn Charles, Ronald Griffiths. By around 1955 the new clubhouse was complete and the 1st XI (seen in the photograph) are, left to right, back row: G. Cawood, G. Charles, R. James. E. Morris, I. Morris, K. Charles, B. Jenkins, B. Salmon, D. Humphreys, I. Rees. Front row, kneeling: C. Phillips, A. Davies, R. Stephens, R. Griffiths. Standing amongst the players is Canon Keble-Williams, the vicar of Llanrhian.

The Reverend Canon T. Owen Phillips with his Church Lads Brigade Club in their 'official' uniform in 1940. As well as being a 'powerful' preacher he devoted a great deal of time to his Youth Club, paying all the expenses including an annual trip to play Swansea Juniors. Left to right, back row: Fred John, Peter Davies, Brian Roberts, Frank Lewis, Peter Price, David Narbett, Leonard Narbett, Dennis John. Front row, seated: Leo Morris, Derek Davies, Dennis Morgan, Jim Davies, David Salmon.

The CLB Football Club with the Revd Canon T. Owen Phillips outside the Beehive Shop, St David's in 1943. Left to right, back row: Alan Preece, G. James, David Narbett, Leonard Narbett. Middle row: Desmond Howells, Neville Evans, Maldive Evans, John Beynon, Dewi Preece. Front row: Dennis Morgan, Les Morris, Jim Davies.

St David's Church Lads Brigade at Mumbles in 1946. Left to right, back row: Minor Canon Victor Jones, Tony Davies, Desmond Howells, John Beynon, David Narbett, Colin Rees, Ieuan Griffiths, Canon T.O. Phillips. Front row, sitting: Richard Lloyd, Ivor Lewis, Dewi Preece, Graham Beer, John Harries.

Six
Ramsey, Whitesands and Carn Llidi

The Island of Ramsey, in the background, is surrounded by rocks known as the 'Bishop and his Clerks'. The Pembrokeshire historian, John Henry Owen, born at Henllys in 1552 wrote that, 'the Bishop and these his Clerkes preache daily doctrine to their winter audience, such poor seafaring men as are forcyd thether by tempest, onlie one thing they are to be commended, they keep residence better then the rest of the cannons of that see are wont to do'.

Lionel Whitehead the Welsh Steel Magnate (inset) had a holiday home at St Justinian and liked the area so much that he bought Ramsey Island as a birthday present for his wife in 1935. He was a very keen naturalist and a member of the RSPB and it was his ambition to see the island farmed efficiently and to enhance its established natural history. Legend has it that on a pilgrimage in 1171 Henry II, who was keen on hawking sent his goshawk in to attack the native peregrine, the goshawk was struck and fell dead at the feet of the king, ever after he had his falcons from Ramsey Island.

Looking across Ramsey Sound to the island from the copper mine which is below Treginnis Farm. The roof of the farmhouse can be seen behind Axe Rock and the farm buildings above on the right. There was a corn mill just to the left of the house which was fed by a small stream which was collected in a mill pond a little further up, the water being released when milling took place. The tidal race can be seen passing through and around the dreaded Bitches reef.

One problem confronted Lionel Whitehead – the access to the island which was disrupted by the force of the water flooding to the north over the Bitches (where the St David's lifeboat came to grief). He approached local contractors, David Thomas and Son to construct a quay between the innermost rock and the island.

The quay that stonemasons Nant James and Bertie Griffiths built for Lionel Whitehead. It was due to the determination of these two stonemasons, having laid the foundation of the quay many times only to find that the force of the tide had carried all away, that the quay was built and it is a tribute to them that sixty years later the quay still stands. At low water access is gained by the steps leading down to the left. Bertie remained on the island to repair the buildings and on the death of Lionel Whitehead, in 1938, Mrs Whitehead offered the tenancy of the island to Bertie. Together with his wife Hannah he made the island a successful farming enterprise.

Hannah Griffiths with her flock of geese above the harbour. From 1939 to 1947 the island was farmed intensively by Bertie, and the fact that it was separate from the mainland interested Sir George Stapleton of the Welsh Agricultural College, Aberystwyth, who experimented with the growing of certain strains of cereal as well as S.100 clover.

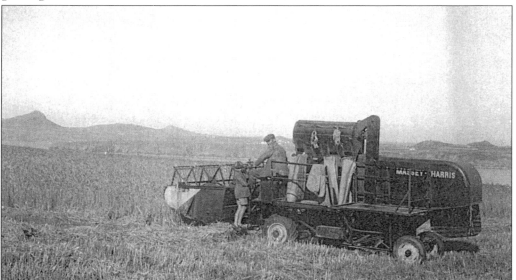

Peter Rowe with one of the first self propelled Massey Harris Combine Harvesters in Pembrokeshire. The combine had to be stripped down, shipped over to the island, and then re-built. In 1947 Bertie Griffiths left the island and took on the tenancy of Lower Treginnis Farm, just over the water. Thus, Peter Rowe with his father from Yorkshire were given the tenancy. Ramsey Sound and the mainland are in the background with Carn Llidi to the left.

Shipping of goods to the island. For many living on an island is a great dream, but when the dream comes true it is very hard work. Cattle have to be hoisted aboard a boat, then driven up the steps of St Justinian, which were designed by Basil Jones, the owner of the Mart Ground in Haverfordwest for the cattle. Each bag of fertiliser has to be handled about six times before it is eventually spread on the land. Coal, fuel, food and a hundred and one things have to be passed hand to hand, hard work indeed!

The Coxswain of the St David's lifeboat Captain William Watts Williams, popularly known as 'Skip' leaving the harbour with some of the men at the end of the season who had been helping on the farm. He knew Ramsey Sound like the 'back of his hand' and ferried people to and from the island for many years. Peter Rowe subsequently bought a large farm near Hayscastle where he is farming to this day.

D. Watts Evans, Bryn Rees and Fred Jeffrey are preparing the beacon to celebrate the Coronation of Queen Elizabeth II in 1953. The Western Sentinel of the Peninsula is Carn Llidi which, at 595ft, towers above the bay and beach at Whitesands. In the past fires were kindled from the summit which were part of a coastal chain to either warn or celebrate some national event as in 1953.

An aptly named postcard entitled 'The End of the Road' showing Whitesands after a gale in the late 1920s with two well known characters of the City, H.L. Davies of Gwynfa and Evans 'Bon Marche' which was the name of his Drapers Shop opposite the City Garage.